Acclaim

"In, *Ledicia's Key*, Baeu's poignant reprise of far-flung family ties, the author strikes centuries of chords across several continents. Here is the full symphony of humanity, played out in the sharps and flats of personal triumphs and political tragedies. The author reaches backwards and forwards through time to remind us of a hard-won intergenerational truth. Such a timely series of stories; about surviving genocide, displacement, armed conflicts, and the madmen of history as we grapple in the present with another modern-day tragedy another wave of invasions, bombings, war crimes and millions of refugees. As these tales so richly prove, ancestry is more than a DNA test. It is the preservation of wisdom and the prevention of amnesia."

Cynthia F. Davidson, author of *The Importance of Paris*

———

"*Ledicia's Key* is a moving generational biography and a wonderful historical romantic thriller. The author is able to express feelings so deeply that one feels them as well. There are narrow escapes, chilling and tragic losses. The sweeping story and gorgeous locations would make a powerful mini-series."

Mark W. Hammond, Emmy winner,
Directors Guild Member, and
author of *"M in the Demon Realm"* Trilogy

———

"Nachmias-Baeu is such is a wonderful writer. She offers a smooth ride that provokes feelings and thoughts. Her sentence structure and word use, like yeast, give rise to a hearty bread."

Bill Seymour,
writer for *The Independent, The Narragansett Times, The Standard Times* and *South County Life Magazine.*

———

"I couldn't stay away from reading *Ledicia's Key* and so was up till 5 a.m. You know how that happens when a book calls to you. My eyes are now on strike. Some more compresses and eye drops are in my immediate future. I LOVE LOVE LOVE LOVE this book, the story, her writing and imagery, and language. I can't wait to give it to some friends."

Chaiya Zalles,
Former Community College Instructor, PreSchool Director, and
Montessori Teacher Trainer

———

"War comes in a variety of guises: some of such magnitude that they grab the headlines, while others are fought in smaller spaces, for lesser gains and hardly a mention is made of them. Within her lens focused on the latter perspective, *Ledicia's Key* tracks a family through centuries. Baeu gives readers a view offered with breadth and depth as she treats their struggles to survive, their loves and losses, their moral ambiguities in a manner that could only come to life in the deft hands and with the intimate knowledge of an outstanding writer such as Baeu."

Gene McKee, M.D., author of *DOC*,
From *Bloodletting to Binary* and *The Girl from Donegal*

"Kin – Relations - Blood – Tribe – Clan – Folk – Lineage: perhaps there are so many words for the bonds that tie family because they have the power to link generations for centuries. *Ledicia's Key*, Yvette Nachmias-Baeu's fourth book, is built around her main character's hunger – a quest to track family from the Spanish Inquisition to modern day. Despite genetics in common, or perhaps because of it, the diversity of her character's family becomes apparent when we meet Generals and shopkeepers, royalty and commoners as each layer of the mystery of family genealogy gets revealed. For anyone pulled by the attraction of their family tree - *Ledicia's Key* ought to be on your bookshelf."

I. Michael Grossman, author of *Coming to Terms with Aging,*
Shrinkwarpped, The Power, Mike the Mouse,
Poems in Disappearing Ink, and *The Realm.*

LEDICIA'S KEY

THE SEARCH FOR FAMILY THROUGH SIX CENTURIES

YVETTE NACHMIAS-BAEU

Publisher's Information

Author contact: ynb.author@gmail.com
Website and blog: yvettenachmiasbaeu.com

ISBN 978-1-953080-26-4
Library of Congress Control Number: 2022909028
© 2022 by Yvette Nachmias-Baeu

EBookBakery

Photos: Map of Ottoman Empire, Atilim Gunes Baydin, Public domain, via Wikimedia Commons

Cover: Sandro Bottecilli, Portrait of a Young Woman, circa 1480

Author's photo: courtesy of Hank Benson

TABLE OF CONTENTS

The Letter 1
Beka's Decision 5
Entering Sofia 11
The Key 26
Messenger for the King 36
The Next Day 46
Leaving Castile 54
Ledicia and Isaiah 61
Emerging Heroes 67
The Dinner 77
The Painting 84
Goodbye Bulgaria 90
Margot 94
Rachael's Letter 108
Baby Rebekah 110
The Death of Ledicia 116
Michael Returns 120
The Woman in the Park 125
The Hills of Edirne 130
Is There More 140
Paper-making and News Sheets 148
Isaiah, Simca, Edward 151
Ariel's Horse 158
The Other Davids 168
Hugo and The Jewish Brigade 172
"A Man From a Time Gone By". 179
Reunion 184
Other Books by the Author 192
About the Author 195

ACKNOWLEDGMENTS

There are always countless people to thank when one takes on the task of writing a book. I have to thank all the historians who have written about the times, countries and people that are part of this narrative. My unwavering thanks go out to the people who have taken the time to read and comment on this book and give sound encouragement and advise. To all of them, who I name here, I am very grateful: Chaiya Zalles, Mark Hammond, I. Michael Grossman, Theresa Schimmel, Relly Davidson, Cynthia Davidson, Camilla Lee, Gene McKee, Jane McCarthy, Gene Kincaid, Bill Seymour, Tina Kennedy and Joyce Fingerut. And a special nod to the women in the Circle of Five—you know who you are.

In particular I want to thank my late cousin Dr. Jack Nachmias who spent years working on the history of his own family and to Panio Kisselov, who wrote a book about his life which made it possible to understand how it was to live during the second World War and the post war years in Bulgaria.

Dedication

To all the people who have been forced out of their country and been made immigrants. To those that stayed behind to fight for their country and all the people who have been brutally killed for no reason except they wanted to remain free. I dedicate this book to the country of Ukraine and its remarkable people for whom my heart is bleeding.

CHARACTERS

MAIN CHARACTERS
Rebekah (Beka) Avraham	Principal
Dr. Michael Petrov	Principal

BEKA'S IMMEDIATE FAMILY
Sultana David Avraham	Beka's Mother, wife of Jacob
Jacob Avraham	Beka's Father, husband of Sultana
Reva Avraham	Beka's Sister

BEKA'S GRANDPARENTS
Joseph Avraham	Paternal Grandfather
Vivenza (Vivachi) Avraham	Paternal Grandmother
Samuel David	Maternal Grandfather
Zora David	Maternal Grandmother

ANCESTORS
Ledicia Serrano Avraham	1st Person known in the Avraham family
Naftali Serrano	Ledicia's Father
Isaiah Avraham	Ledicia's Husband
Rebekah Avraham	Deceased daughter of Ledicia & Isaiah
Naftali Avraham	Son of Ledicia & Isaiah
Armand Avraham	Son of Ledicia & Isaiah
Simca Avraham West	Daughter of Ledicia & Isaiah
Edward West	Husband of Simca
Pantelay Kristov*	Petya's Grandfather
Rafael Binyamin Avraham	Beka's Great Great Paternal Grandfather
Binyamin Rafael Avraham*	Beka's Great Paternal Grandfather
Ariel David	15th Century relation to Beka's mother
Hyram David	17th Century relation to Beka's mother

PATERNAL UNCLES, AUNTS, COUSINS
Asher Avraham	Beka's Uncle, Brother of Jacob
Charlo Avraham	Beka's Uncle, Brother of Jacob
Hanna Avraham	Beka's Cousin, Charlo's daughter
Lize Avraham Bohor	Beka's Aunt, Sister of Jacob
Izak Bohor	Beka's Uncle, Husband of Lize
Hugo Bohor	Beka's cousin, son of Lize & Izak
Gina Bohor Nissimov	Beka's cousin, daughter of Lize & Izak
Benjamin Bohor	Beka's cousin, son of Lize & Izak
Gregor Kristov*	Beka's Uncle, Father of Petya
Irina Avraham Kristov	Beka's Aunt, Mother of Petya

Petya Kristov	Beka's Cousin, Son of Gregor & Irina
Maria Kristov	Beka's Cousin, Daughter of Gregor & Irina
Rachael Avraham	Second Cousin once removed
Bastein Avraham	Husband of Rachael Avraham
Elise Avraham	Beka's second cousin
Ruth Avraham	Grandmother to Elise
Elias Avraham	Grandfather to Elise
Bella Avraham	Beka's Great Aunt, mother of Carl
Carl Avraham	Son of Bella, cousin to Jacob

MATERNAL AUNTS, UNCLES, COUSINS

Reuben David	Beka's Uncle, Brother of Sultana
Linda David	Beka's Aunt, Wife of Victor
Serina David	Beka's cousin. Daughter of Victor & Linda
Flor David Avraham	Beka's Aunt, Sister of Sultana
Benno Avraham	Beka's Uncle, Husband of Flor
Theo David	Beka's Uncle, Brother of Sultana
Vicki	Beka's Cousin, daughter of Theo
Margot Davoud	Daughter of Zitia/Victor. 1st Cousin to Sultana
Danielle and Fanny	Daughters of Margot Davoud
Zitia Davoud	Aunt to Sultana, Mother of Margot
Victor Davoud	Uncle to Sultana, Father of Margot

MINOR CHARACTERS

Minka	Nanny to Beka and Reva
Mr. Lazarov	Concierge at 22 Krakra St.
Efron Hazan	Ledicia Serrano's employer
Lee	Beka's early boyfriend
Constance	Michael's brief affair

ACTUAL HISTORICAL FIGURES

King Boris	King of Bulgaria - 1919- 1943
Boghan Filov	Prime Minister of Bulgaria 1940-1945
Georgi Kisselov*	Negotiated with the US for the King - WWII
Pantelay Kisselov*	General -won back Tutrakan in 1912
Ivan Vedar	Scholar who helped save Ruschuk 1877
Binyamin Raphael Nachmias*	Saved Ruschuk with Ivan Vedar 1877

*In this book Gregor Kristov is actually Georgi Kisselov
*In this book, Pantelay Kristov is actually Pantelay Kisselov
*In the book, Binyamin Raphael Avraham is actually Binyamin Raphael Nachmias

The Balkans

The Ottoman Empire

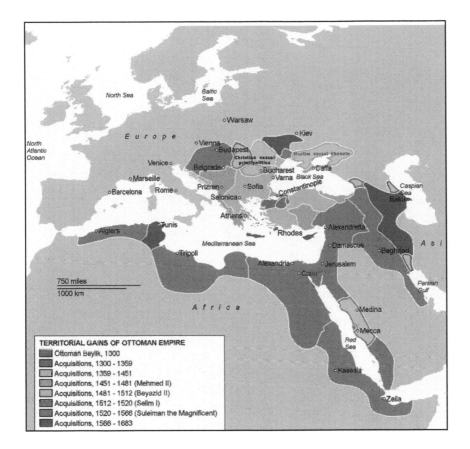

North Sea

Baltic Sea

North Atlantic Ocean

Europe

○Warsaw

○Vienna

○Kiev

○Budapest

Christian vassal principalities

Muslim vassal khanate

Venice○

Belgrade○

○Bucharest

○Caffa

Marseille○

Prizren○

○Sofia

○Varna Black Sea

Caspian Sea

○Barcelona Rome○

Salonica○

Constantinople

Baku○

Athens○

A s i

Rhodes

○Alexandretta

Algiers○

Tunis○

Mediterranean Sea

○Damascus

○Baghdad

Tripoli○

Alexandria○

Jerusalem

○Cairo

Persian Gulf

750 miles

1000 km

Africa

○Medina

○Mecca

Red Sea

○Kassala

○Zeila

TERRITORIAL GAINS OF OTTOMAN EMPIRE

- Ottoman Beylik, 1300
- Acquisitions, 1300 - 1359
- Acquisitions, 1359 - 1451
- Acquisitions, 1451 - 1481 (Mehmed II)
- Acquisitions, 1481 - 1512 (Beyazid II)
- Acquisitions, 1512 - 1520 (Selim I)
- Acquisitions, 1520 - 1566 (Suleiman the Magnificent)
- Acquisitions, 1566 - 1683

1

THE LETTER

A THIN BROWN ENVELOPE lies on the floor by her front door. There's a note in red marker on the front, saying, "sorry, this was delivered to me instead of to you," and signed by the man living upstairs.

Rebekah carries it to the kitchen and drops it on the counter while she brews a small pot of coffee. Now wide awake, she slides the envelope towards her noticing the postmark and stamps are foreign. Her address is written in a perfectly formed and pointed script, much the way most Europeans still write. Handwriting, she muses, has not deteriorated there as much as it has in America. Looking at the postmark more carefully she notices it's from Bulgaria. Disappointed that the letter is written in a Cyrillic alphabet and alarmed that it looks official, she sets out to find someone who can translate it, worries it won't be an easy task. Bulgarian is not a common language, spoken or studied, in this backwater or anywhere, for that matter. But it is a college town so she hopes she will be successful.

As luck will have it, she locates a professor at the University who speaks Bulgarian. Encouraged, she calls and asks him for his help. He is brisk in his response, hurried in his speech, but is willing to meet Rebekah and look at the letter.

In the meantime, she learns that Dr. Michael Petrov is a chaired professor of European and Slavic History. Even with this pedigree, it seems to her, he has all the grace of a herd of buffalo. Put-off by his manner, she tries to ignores her first impression because she is told by one of his students that his courses are well attended, his lectures interesting forays into literature, history and culture. Beka likes what she hears and decides to forgive his telephone manner.

Today she plans to meet Petrov at a local coffee shop near the campus at four in the afternoon.

Checking her watch frequently, she watches the heavy rain come down, exasperated by how slowly time is going by. Finally at three-thirty, she makes sure the letter is in her bag, wraps a scarf around her neck, pulls on her gloves, grabs her umbrella and walks the five blocks to their meeting place.

The Coffee Club is a busy hangout at this hour. Beka notices that some students are sitting around, eyes fixed on their open computers, a half-empty cup of cold coffee next to them. They've probably been here for hours. Other students sit together at crowded tables engaged in heated conversations that range from the serious to the raucous. There are couples looking at each other with the promise of romance in their eyes, others with the tired realization that theirs is winding down. The crush of people, the smell of freshly roasting coffee beans amidst the smell of wet wool and unwashed bodies is a bit overwhelming and Rebekah wonders why the professor chose this place to meet.

Looking around, it dawns on her that she has no idea what the professor looks like. She worries that they might not find a table away from the din or a table at all. Planting herself in front of the counter next to the croissants, she surveys the room when someone taps her on the shoulder. Professor Petrov has figured out who she is. Of course, he has. She is considerably older than the average patron.

"Ms. Avraham? I have a table. Follow me."

As he guides her to the table, she sees there are already two cups of coffee waiting. He says apologetically that he hopes he chose the right kind.

"I haven't added anything. Do you prefer it sweetened?"

"That›s fine," she says somewhat distracted by Petrov's warm manner. "I take it black."

"So," he says. "How can I help you?" He isn't wasting any time on small talk or introductions. Rebekah is reminded of her knee-jerk reaction to him. He isn't anything like what she imagined. He's about the same age as she is and has a deeply carved and interesting face. Though he is probably in his sixties, he seems a youthful man and to her surprise, seems polite. She fully expected to meet a grizzled old man with a three-day growth, a wrinkled collar and cigarette ash on the sleeve of his shapeless overcoat. But he is clean-shaven, sportily dressed and has all his hair—a peppery mix of black and grey. His eyes are a warm hazel which seem to give off a sadness that his gentle smile accentuates.

"Dr. Petrov, I received this letter from Bulgaria. It looks official and I can't read it. Can you translate it? Oh," she adds, as she extends her hand, "How do you do, I am Rebekah, but people call me Beka. Thanks for meeting me.'

"Please, call me Michael." His English accent is curious. It's a mix of something else she can't put her finger on.

"By the way, are you Bulgarian, Rebekah?"

"Well, I was born there but I came to America when I was very young."

"I see. Well then, may I see the letter?"

Hastily taking it out of her bag, she hands it to him, noticing that he has nice hands and manicured nails. She watches as he scans the envelope before removing the letter, feeling her heart beating just a little faster than usual. When he looks up at her he smiles and says,

"The letter is from the Bulgarian Housing Authority informing you that an apartment belonging to your family before the war is now back in your sister Reva and your hands. The government has released it. Currently, there are no tenants living there, and you are in control of how you would like to use or dispose of it."

"Really!" Rebekah blurts out in astonishment. We own property in Bulgaria?"

"Yes—in the city of Sofia on...let's see... Ulitsa 22 Krakra. That means street, by the way. Here I will write down the name of the official and the department you are to get in touch with. Of course, you may have some difficulty as English is still not commonly spoken there, except for students, and you must fill out this form. If you need help, just let me know."

She thanks Michael profusely. They sit there awhile longer in an uncomfortable silence, taking a few more sips of coffee before they simultaneously get up, saying in unison, they must be getting on. Beka laughs nervously and again extends her hand to say goodbye. They leave the shop, walking away in different directions. After taking a few steps. Beka turns around and watches Dr. Petrov amble down the street. Just as she does this, he stops to light a cigarette and turns around looking in Beka's direction. Awkwardly, they both smile and wave to each other.

2
BEKA'S DECISION

BEKA'S HANDS PLUNGE into the hot dish water. Ah, she cries. "There you are, you little devil." She pulls out a small silver spoon she found years ago when clearing out her parents' apartment after her father's death. It survived years of use from one continent to another. The handle has the worn monogram of a family she never knew. It is among the few things left that link her to the family.

"It would not be right for me to lose you in such a clumsy way—down the drain!" She dries it off and puts it in the drawer with the embroidered linens and lace table scarves her father sent her after her mother 's death. They are beautiful, though she has never found a reason to use them. Her own furnishings do not lend themselves to the dainty refinement of a time gone by. Once in America, her mother rarely had a chance to use them either. Still, they were carefully stored in a linen closet, too beautiful to be thrown away, but too fragile to be used. They represent the treasured relics made by her mother's hand that will probably be lost once she passes on. Her son will find no reason to keep them.

"I may be the last one. It could stop with me." All Beka's random thoughts are spoken aloud as if there is someone in the room. A habit that began a few years ago, after her husband's death. Her early retirement left her even more alone. She finds herself living in a silent home, with less responsibilities and more time on her hands.

"You're a silly old bat, just quit it."

One thing she does not want to do is slip into the habits ascribed to the elderly. Still, the quiet of her rooms often wear on her. She leans over and turns on the radio. It always calms her and takes up the silence. She hears the familiar phrasing of Mozart's Sonata *#11* which can lift anyone's dreary mood. Why, she wonders, are the vague feelings of ancestry and surnames visiting her so often lately?"

"When my generation dies, will my name disappear? Maybe it doesn't matter. It's what happens when a family produces mostly girls. The pool dries up."

The practice of taking the name of the father means that none of the family's progeny will carry her last name into the future. It has already been rearranged from its biblical origins. Even her sister legally changed it, not wanting to be ethnically identified.

Unclear why these thoughts stick in her mind now, Rebekah, is aware that she never felt completely attached to the name. Over the years it had reconfigured itself to accommodate different languages and different countries. Never feeling possessive of it, she recently began to recognize how much history it carries. All her life, it produced confusion as most everyone stumbled on its pronunciation and questioned its origin. Yet, she stubbornly kept it after marriage, but never spent much time wondering why. She could have dropped it and taken her husband's name or any other for that matter. Why not her mother's maiden name, David? Wouldn't that have been simpler?

In her younger years, she rarely thought about her background. Lately, it has begun to feel important. Does it have to do with the letter she stowed away in her desk?

Perhaps now, on the cusp of what is likely her final years, she recognizes, with a degree of sadness that something important went missing from her life precisely because she never really felt completely attached to her family, never curious enough to learn about them.

Mozart's music reminds her of her mother. Though they both loved classical music, Beka did not inherit her mother's passion for opera, vividly recalling the Saturday afternoons during opera season. The family was hurried out of the apartment so her mother could listen, undisturbed, to the Saturday afternoon broadcast from the Metropolitan Opera House. The only part of an opera Beka liked and could identify, were the major arias that punctuated the drama of the story. Otherwise, it always sounded like singsong and bellowing, accompanied by bad-acting.

Admittedly, her mother had traits she's glad she did not inherit, but why hadn't she acquired some of her finer qualities? She spent her youth believing in her uniqueness, to mitigate her self-consciousness. Beka never wondered what inclinations, dispositions, and attributes were given to her and which ones were not. She was told often enough that she looked like her mother's side of the family. Why then did she not have her mother's blue eyes? She would have liked to have blue eyes, but her own eyes are an everyday brown, like those on her father's side.

"I do have my mother's tall frame, and thankfully, though prominent enough, I did not inherit the Avraham nose!"

Her estrangement seems even more pronounced as she turns the pages of the photograph albums she found stowed away in her bedroom closet. Taking them off the shelf, she turns the pages, examining every one of the old photographs. Stopping to examine a photo of her young mother, she realizes, once again that her youthful mother, Sultana, was a beautiful woman. She dressed so elegantly. She always knew how to put outfits together that flattered her. Beka appreciates style when seen on others but lacks the ability to create her own. She is more comfortable wearing jeans, always choosing dark or neutral colors, consistently failing to find the right thing to wear, missing the mark on special occasions, even her own wedding.

"My feet are a bit too big for the stylish shoes that never seem to be produced in my size. All the nicest styles are cut in a size range that don't fit me. They seem to purposely style larger sizes in plain less attractive and certainly unimaginative designs. I panic when I must "dress-up.""

One thing she admired about her mother were her dancing fingers. She was able to sew, knit, crochet and embroider. It was always assumed that all females were born with this innate ability. Yet these were skills Beka did not possess. This utter lack, she figured, had a lot to do with being left-handed and reassured herself that there would be plenty of opportunities to rise above these deficiencies. In fact, her goal was to do something really dramatic, though she had no idea what that might be.

"My disinterest was genuine. It came from an ideological principle of gender- stereotyping, but was I only accommodating what I lacked?"

7

There is very little of her father's traits she recognizes in herself. She is grateful for that, though she knows she is being too harsh. He was a man that worried about things, large and small. Relegating special duties to himself–it was his way of controlling life–like the amount of air allowed to sift into the apartment, keenly aware of the potential hazard of drafts. He derived strength by controlling the small things in life—how loud the radio was, when dinner must be served, what coats his children should wear. That helped to ameliorate all the things he couldn't control. He did have a quirky ability to engineer and fix things, loved the outdoors, and had a sense of duty to his family that was admirable—and in spite of himself, he could be amusing when he remembered how.

She did feel close to her parents but strained at the connection that bound them together. There had always been an overwhelming wish to venture out, independent of family considerations. They couldn't believe she gave up a nursing career after only two years to try her hand at the theater, which had always been her underlying desire. While she had a dramatic look, she worried that her height and ethnic appearance would deny her many leading roles, but then she was far more attracted to the classics, and off-beat authors like, Brecht and Genet, than the more realistic plays of the time. She amusingly held to the notion that she'd been hatched from an egg that accidentally found its way into this family. She tried to understand the world outside of hers, which often frightened her, and yet she had to find out who she really was other than merely a daughter.

Except for a few half-remembered anecdotes from the infrequent stories her parents spoke of, Beka has few stories to grab onto, so it is hard to align herself to the parts of her heritage that had deeper roots. She was uninterested in the lives connected to her own before she was born. She was, up till now, willing to remain unattached to her history.

Now in the disquieting moments of her enforced solitude, her husband buried five years ago, far away memories begin to return like the smell of old books or the hallways of her elementary school. Her blood, she realizes, is part of other people's blood. Her being and body constructed from the souls that landed on earth long ago. Who were these people? What were their stories? Could she climb upon the shoulders of all those that had come before her, become an integral part of the world she inherited? Was her life bumping up against the branches of a very old tree that is dying? Would there be new trees sprouting from the old tree's seedlings? Beka begins to feel a keen desire to discover what she never till now bothered to know. Where did the name Avraham originate and on how many pages of history known or never recorded did it occupy?

"The letter!" That›s the source of all these churning thoughts. For weeks Beka has avoided the content of the letter and what it might signify. Now she thinks of little else. Running to her desk, she hopes she correctly remembers that she tossed it in the drawer after her meeting with the Professor Petrov—Michael. That was his name, right? Perhaps this letter was a messenger, a not-so-gentle push, and the reason for her recent obsession about family.

It's been a while since her meeting with the professor. Screwing up her courage, Beka picks up the phone and calls him. Happily, he remembers her and politely asks how she is. Still not clear about what she is about to ask, she blurts out,

"I have decided to take a trip to Bulgaria, and I wonder if you would be willing to, I mean, would you be free to accompany me to Bulgaria— actually go with me?"

There is a long silence which feels deafening. Feverish with her idea, she waits impatiently for his answer. In order to fill the silence, she continues;

"I know it's a crazy notion. You don't know me and I certainly don't know you. I have no idea what has possessed me to ask, but I feel I must go and you are the only one I can think of that knows Bulgaria and speaks the language. You even said you would help. I want to learn more about my family."

Beka waits but there is still silence at the other end, which doesn't stop her for long.

"So…here is all I know about myself. I am a Sephardic Jew. Well my family is, and I believe we came from a family that was part of the migration out of Spain because of the Inquisition of 1492. My parents spoke Ladino as their primary language, but they did not pass it on to me. There must be more to know. I want to know more!" Breathlessly she continues. "I know it's nuts, but I am asking anyway."

Finally, as if Petrov has finally taken all the time he needs, says,

"As a matter of fact, I have a sabbatical coming up after this semester and I was considering a visit to Bulgaria to do some research. I've been wondering how things must be changing since the breakup of the Soviet Union. You've given me an idea. I'll give this a bit more thought."

Later that same day he calls her, saying simply that he will go with her. They suggest meeting again to figure out what they both want to do. Her *ask* she is sure, will be the easiest part of what is in store for her, and the *ask* was hard enough.

22 Krakra Street, Sofia Bulgaria

3

ENTERING SOFIA

AFTER MICHAEL AGREES to go to Bulgaria with her, they meet a few times to talk about her project and to fill out the forms sent to her. Each time, Beka begins to feel slightly more comfortable with Michael, as he is straightforward, helpful, likable, and seems genuinely interested in her project.

She checks and double-checks every item on her list. Her bags are finally packed. Deciding what is important to take and what is unnecessary is harder than she thought it would be, particularly as she prefers traveling light. Harder still, because she might be there for a long time, but even that isn't a sure thing.

Glancing at her watch frequently, she peers through the window, impatiently waiting for Michael to arrive in a cab. She is finding it hard to overcome the anxiety that has been building ever since she asked Michael to come with her.

"Damn, I'm so nervous. I must calm down. This is the craziest thing I've ever done, and hell, I hate flying!"

She remembers when flying was a special adventure. There was such excitement about catching a plane and traveling to a distant place. It was classy and special and people dressed for the occasion. Now people are in clothes they normally wear to mow their lawns. In the past few years, flying has become a nuisance as well as a necessity. If she had a choice and nothing but time, she'd rather travel by ocean liner or freighter or train. But everyone including herself, is always in a hurry. The only good thing about traveling by air, Beka insists, is finally arriving at one's destination. The in-between time is an ordeal you simply have to endure. The minimalist seats they expect you to fit into makes her clinical, but at the same time the engineered miniature designs of everything on the aircraft fascinate her.

The first leg of the journey creates some nervous moments with plane delays and a rocky crossing. There is a tedious three-hour wait for their next connection in the chaotic Heathrow airport, but at least it gives them time to stretch out before being confined in another aircraft, stuffed in spaces that might accommodate a child of ten. Relieved to land in Sofia, she is happy to leave the maw of the airport and relax in the roomy rented car. She bathes in the luxury of being able to stretch out her legs as they drive through Sofia towards her newly acquired apartment.

Staring out of the car's window, Beka feels an excitement that over-rides her exhaustion and her airplane grievances. There is a pull towards this foreign city, a part of her life she was too young to remember.

Driving towards the apartment, a map in her hands, she sees two parks are flanking Krakra Street. When they pass a large building nestled

in one of the parks, Michael points out Sofia University where he went
to school.

"My family left Bulgaria when I was four and settled in England.
When I graduated from secondary school, I was looking for a reason to
return so, I chose Sofia University."

Beka's interest is aroused. Up till now, she hasn't heard Michael
talk about himself at all. "Wasn't Bulgaria still under the thumb of the
Communists?"

"Yes, it was, but since I had dual citizenship, it was possible to
matriculate. Being interested in history I thought this might be a good
place to take my undergraduate studies. Unfortunately, the four years
I spent here were curious and hard under the communist regime, but
there were hints of an intellectual thaw."

Beka turns to look at Michael, glad that he is beginning to talk to
her about parts of his life.

"Cultural and literary discussions were beginning to flower, not just
at school but everywhere. Nonetheless we still felt uneasy about voicing
our opinions. While I was there, the Hungarian Revolution erupted and
the Russians clamped down again. They weren't taking the chance of
weakening their grip on the country. Once again, it was purged of art and
intellectual discussions. People, particularly students, were discouraged
from becoming independent thinkers. I was pretty relieved to return to
England, once I graduated."

"So, you were here during the Communist days? Another of its
historically difficult times. I see a lot of remnants left by the Communists. I'm surprised you chose to do your undergraduate studies here."

"I was, shall we say, just curious enough. But as it turned out, it
wasn't easy or much fun."

"This is a pretty neighborhood though, isn't it?" While he nods in
the affirmative, her remarks unintentionally stop Michael from any
further conversation.

Finding a parking space in front of her building, Beka steps out of
the car trying to digest the reality that she is standing in front of the
building where her life began. That door is the same door her family
exited years ago, not knowing if they would ever see this city again. Her

mother never did. Her father returned for a visit when he was old and frail. Her sister visited when she turned forty, but this is the first time Beka has been back. While her sister is a joint owner of the apartment, Reva has little interest in it. Mostly, she complains that it is too far away from her California home and she is quite sure she will never set foot in an airplane again. Beka, she insists, is free to do what she wants with it, as long as she pays the costs. Should Beka decide to sell it, they agreed to share in the spoils. Beka wonders if she will still feel like a stranger here, as she has all her life, or if this episode will change her sense of detachment.

December, 1940
22 Krakra Street, Sofia, Bulgaria

Reva and Rebakah
Reva and Rebekah

Frightened by the threat of war and caught-up in Europe's rising hatred towards Jews, Jacob, Sultana and their two children hurriedly walk out of their building's front door carrying four suitcases for the hazardous journey that will take them to America. They dare not contemplate what this will mean. Are they leaving temporarily or forever? While this is not the time to think about that, it is hard to avoid. They only know they cannot stay. Sultana's aging mother refuses to leave and her sister, Flor, has no intention of going anywhere. Sultana is thankful that they will be together, but frightened that they might be in danger and that this may be the last time she ever sees them.

There haven't yet been bombing raids in the country, but the climate around the capital is tense. When Bulgaria signed the Tripartite Pact, allying itself with Nazi Germany and the Axis powers, it should have been a warning to Jews that they might be in danger. Rebekah's uncle Ascher had already emigrated to America, fearing what was likely to happen and suggested, a year ago, that it was not safe to stay in Europe. Jacob took his brother's warning seriously and begins preparations to leave the country. Because of his financial position, he is able to make travel arrangements, First, he transfers money to Ascher's bank in American and exchanges enough lira for their trip. He applies for visas and passports. The last thing he does is buy crosses for his children and Sultana. He then has his daughters baptized in the Congregational Church. But they leave all their furnishings, rugs and painting, hoping they will be able to retrieve them one day. After many weeks, the final arrangements have been made.

Ripples of anti-Semitism begin to impact them. Even Minka, always a faithful and loving nanny to Rebekah and her older sister Reva, seems to be sympathizing with the Germans. Some of her nuanced remarks worry Sultana, who wonders if this simple country woman, always an integral part of her family, has fallen victim to the current propaganda. Tension around the house is palpable. Sultana must have a talk with Minka. Sitting her down over a cup of tea while the children take their nap, the room bright with the afternoon sun, the specter of what may come, still not clear, she asks Minka directly if she no longer wishes to work for a Jewish family. Confronting the question, Minka at first protests, then she breaks down, ashamed of her betrayal, and begins to cry. It is clear that she's allowed herself to be influenced by her neighbors. She promises to remain loyal to the Avraham family. Nothing more is said during the next weeks, while the family, prepares for their departure.

Jacob is able to book a Greek ship moored in the Port of Lisbon. They will travel to Genoa by train, then fly from there to Portugal. All they take, apart from clothes, jewelry, a photo album, money and their papers, are two feather duvets that were part of Sultana's trousseau, thinking they might protect them against the cold should they become stranded.

On the morning of their departure, Minka helps the family by carrying the luggage downstairs to the building's foyer. Returning to the apartment, she wipes her eyes from time to time to brush away tears that threaten to escape. Sultana comes up beside her holding a large box.

"Minka, this is for you." Minka blinks and screws up her face, taking on a questioning look. She hesitates to take the box.

"Please take it. It's my wedding gown."

Minka opens the box slowly and strokes the beautiful crepe silk. She never owned anything so luxurious. It takes a moment before she is able to speak. Then in a hoarse whisper, manages to say, "Thank you, Madame Sultana, it's beautiful."

"Perhaps you will wear it when you get married. Maybe it will remind you of us. I know we will not forget you."

As they gather the rest of their belongings, Jacob and Sultana shake her hand and the children grab at Minka's skirt and hug her. Minka stays in the apartment looking through the open window waving good-bye. Sultana looks up at the window where Minka has stationed herself, hoping this will not be the last time she sees her. When Minka sees Sultana's face through the taxi's window, she lifts the gown to her cheek, waves and throws the departing family many kisses.

Moving away from their street, neither Jacob or Sultana look back. The taxi takes them to the train station where they are pushed and shoved among a crush of people. A black train roars into the station almost hidden by clouds of smoke frightening Reva who grabs onto her mother's hand. Her mother looks down at her oldest daughter and picks her up.

"Reva, we are going to take that train, but there is nothing to be afraid of. That train is taking us to Italy."

Reva hides her face in her mother's coat, "But it's very noisy and it's on fire," Reva whimpers.

Rebekah looks up at her father's worried face and grabs his hand. "Papa, there's nothing to be afraid of. That train will take us to Italy."

Somewhere along the way, Reva loses the storybook that Sultana brought to read to them, so the children are restless and the journey seems very long. The train stops when it reaches the Italian border, soldiers enter the train. They seem to be taking a very long time, examining their papers and Jacob is nervous that the baptismal papers and the crosses they are wearing will not pass inspection. When the soldiers move on without comment, Jacob and Sultana look at each other in silence. Once arriving in Genoa, not yet settled in their hotel room, the loud whining sound of air raid sirens begin. Hearing planes overhead, they crawl hand-in-hand down the dark staircase towards a shelter. Rebekah is confused. Her bladder empties into the diaper her mother remembered to put on her. She is very quiet and obedient, though she and her sister are frightened. The shelter is poorly lit and damp. Around them are families with crying children. There are single men and a few women. Some are quiet, staring into the darkness. Others are drinking wine and talking in whispers. Reva, always the most gregarious one in the family asks a little girl they are sitting next to if she wants to play a game. The little girl doesn't understand Reva who is speaking Bulgarian, and crawls closer to her mother. Twenty minutes later an all-clear siren allows them to go back to their room.

By morning, having slept poorly, they prepare for the next leg of the trip. With all their baggage in tow, they take another taxi to the airport. Long lines and confusion greet them as Sultana and Jacob deal with tickets and luggage, keeping the children close while trying to remain calm. Reva feels her parent's nervousness and instinctively takes Rebeckah's hand and begins to sing a folksong Minka taught her. Once they finally take off, their parents begin to relax until Reva becomes airsick.

Jacob and Sultana know this is still only the beginning. The longest part of the journey to America is still ahead of them. When they arrive at the port in Lisbon, they learn that the Greek ship they booked passage on will be unable to leave the harbor because Greece has just entered the war. Tired and disheartened, Jacob does everything in his power not to panic. By nature a nervous man, he looks at Sultana who is trying to put on a brave face but he sees the worried lines on her face.

"We haven't come all this way to turn back. We will find a ship."

He hugs Sultana and walks away leaving his wife and the girls sitting in the crowded, cold waiting area. The girls are hungry and Sultana is almost in tears. Luckily, she brought figs and crackers with her which keep her daughters occupied. When Sultana sees Jacob running towards them holding up some papers, she burst into tears. He looks triumphant as he tells them he managed to exchange their tickets for the last four places on a Portuguese ship heading for New York, which is already boarding. Relief washes over Sultana's face and they hurriedly make their way to the ship.

After the eerie hotel in Genoa, and having been on their best behavior during the long train trip, the plane ride and the long wait at the dock, Reva and Rebekah run wildly around the upper deck of the ship and let go of pent-up energy. They both love the open space and smell of fresh air. Sultana, fearing they will fall overboard, chases them all around the upper deck of the ship. Following close behind them, she finally corrals her children whose energy and emotions have turned them into little hellions. Out-of-breath, she grabs the sisters and for the remainder of the trip only lets them out of the cabin when they promise to hold her hand.

Reaching New York in four and half days, the ship passes the Statue of Liberty heading for the Manhattan docks. The people gather on deck and let out an inaudible exhale. The awed silence among the passengers soon becomes a timid cheer which grows louder and louder. When the boat docks, Jacob's brother Asher is waiting for them. A transcendental feeling of relief at seeing a familiar face overcomes Jacob, but the ache of leaving his country and the fear of what comes next is heavy on his mind. Sultana and Jacob understand they will have to negotiate a whole new world and learn a new language. While it is comforting to spend the next few days with Asher and his family, Jacob worries about finding a place to live and a way to earn a living. Asher helps them find a residential hotel on the West Side of Manhattan. Dazed and bewildered, Rebekah's parents feel the sorrow of their world ending and the blossoming hope of a new beginning.

22 Krakra St. Bulgaria
January, 2003

"Michael, I don't know a word of Bulgarian and only a few in Spanish." My parents spoke Ladino most of the time, particularly when they spoke to each other, and Bulgarian or German when they were with others. How come you still speak Bulgarian?"

"I was born in Bulgaria. My parents always spoke to us in Bulgarian at home. I am surprised your parents did not."

"I believe they felt it was more important that we become Americans as soon as possible. They were learning English, so they only spoke to us in English."

Beka wonders if being here will open some of the buried moments stuffed in the crevices of her mind. Maybe there will be some genetic memory that will become evident or clues surface which will circle around her family's history.

Standing in front of the apartment building, she doesn't know what to look at first. It is as if she wants to hold off experiencing what she will feel when she finally sees the apartment building. Looking around she knows there must be a park nearby because there are many photographs of her family in a park. Down the street, she notices a swath of green and figures that must be it. She turns abruptly and walks towards it as if she is being pulled by an invisible force. Michael, busy with the luggage, stops, looks around for her, closes the car's trunk and follows her. She crosses the street toward one of the entrances to a park that has at its entrance a large sign. Beka turns to Michael who has breathlessly come up behind her and asks what the sign says:

Doctors' Garden

"Really? I wonder why it's called 'Doctors'?"

"The sign says the park is named for the fallen medics during the Russo-Turkish war of 1877-1878, and there is probably a monument there."

"I bet there are hundreds of monuments strewn all over this city to commemorate all the wars this little country was entangled in! I think this is the park where my mother, sister, and Minka spent our afternoons."

The walkways are wide and inviting, edged with flower beds and shrubs, expansive lawns and trees that Beka has not seen before. Though most of the trees are bare now, she picks off a leaf that is still clinging to a tree and presses it between the folds of a napkin she finds in her handbag. Always fascinated by flowers and trees. It looks like some sort of Horse Chestnut…she'll hold onto it till she can look it up.

"Michael, I have many photographs of my sister and me in this park. I love one in particular. My mother told us it was taken by a soldier who saw the two of us and asked if he might take a picture. My sister, the outgoing one of the two of us, is standing at attention holding my hand. But in that photo, I am bent over hiding my face. It is clear that I am shy and protesting. We were always dressed beautifully, and always alike. It must have been fashionable to do so then. We may have been dressed alike, but the photo paints a clear picture of the difference between my sister and me, though, ironically, of the two of us, I turned out to be far more trusting."

Without thinking, Beka reaches for Michael's arm as they walk back towards the apartment. Michael smiles, surprised by her gesture of familiarity.

When they arrive at the entrance to the building, a man wearing a blue workman's outfit steps outside the front entrance and lights a cigarette. She nudges Michael, prompting him to ask if he works in the building. The man responds with a side-to-side nod of his head. Beka, disappointed, thinks he is saying 'no' not realizing that the gesture means 'yes.' Looking suspiciously at them and their luggage, Michael hands him a document. With an air of uncertainty, the man goes inside and closes the door behind him.

Beka shrugs off the man's attitude and for the first time examines the façade of the building. Based on the photograph her sister sent her many years ago, she observes that what had looked like an uncared-for building, the result of the slagging economy under the Communists, has changed. The big patches of peeling gray stucco have been repaired and there is a coat of fresh paint on its stucco walls. The wooden door has been refinished and a new panel of beveled glass installed. Two potted trees flank the main doorway. There is an upscale wine store to the right of the building and a specialty food store on the left.

When the man returns, he is smiling and rips his cap with a slight bow, hands them a set of keys and formally introduces himself as Mr. Lazarov, the concierge. He asks if they intend to move in. Beka nudges Michael who takes the cue, saying that they will spend a few months here, off and on. The now polite Mr. Lazarov shows them to the stairwell that takes them to the second-floor landing and Beka's apartment.

Before stepping into the flat, Beka wonders if she will recognize anything about it. The front door leads into a generous foyer. Beyond, there is a wide opening into a large living room. Michael walks in ahead of her looking for a place to put their luggage. Entering the living room, she sees French doors on the right that lead into the dining room. She notices a ceramic-tiled hallway just off the dining room. At the end of the hallway is a moderate-size kitchen with dated appliances. Along the hallway, a small room and a bathroom, which must have been meant for the maid. Perhaps, their nanny Minka used it. In the main room, to the left of the living room is another hallway which brings them to a suite of bedrooms and a larger bathroom. Michael goes off in that direction. All the walls are a dingy beige and could use a coat of paint. One thing that strikes her as remotely familiar are the French doors. The apartment has a few pieces of tired furniture, probably left by former tenants. She wonders what happened to her parent's elegant furnishings. Photographs in her parents' albums painted a vivid picture of their Bulgarian life. There is a photo of her sister sitting on top of a round side table covered with an elegant lace tablecloth which stood in front of a large window covered with fancy tasseled curtains. She is reminded of the package her father sent her after her mother died. It contained her mother's needlepoint, lace and embroidered tablecloths, and the hand-made pink satin roses stitched onto satin streamers that were part of her trousseau. These items would suit this apartment. They made sense here in a country so much older than anything in America. She remembers reading with surprise, that Bulgaria is the oldest country in

Europe and the only country that has not changed its name since it was first established in the 7th century.

All her parent's furniture was probably taken by the numerous families that lived here during the Communist era, when apartments were assigned to at least two, often three families. Now there is a plain wooden table and a few mismatched chairs in the dining room. An old lumpy upholstered couch is all that is in the sitting room and each of the bedrooms have iron beds and lamps. It occurs to her, almost as an afterthought, that they will have to find, before this day ends, some bedding and kitchen equipment and food, as the cupboards are bare.

Then a shiver runs down her spine. The apartment feels eerie. The old-world details, parquet floors, ceiling moldings and the decorative plaster-paneled walls are still here but it is as if she can feel what this apartment experienced after they left. She can hear the sound of bombs from American planes and later the whispers of countless strangers, tucked away in various parts of the apartment after the war. The smell, too, is unrecognizable. Opening a window to air out the room, she sits on the couch and stares at this sparsely furnished room and the peeling plaster on the ceiling.

"So, Beka, what do you think?" Looking up at Michael, she sighs. Then absent-mindedly says,

"We will have to buy a few things right away."

Michael offers a suggestion. "Okay, we can do that now. But then let's find a restaurant. I'm very hungry. Then we can get some rest and figure out what to do next." Beka nods mechanically.

Yes, what do we do next? She feels confused! Should they first look up a cousin she believes still lives in the city? That would likely be a good first stop or maybe she would rather take the bus to one of the entrances to the *Vitosha* mountain range that edge the city and hike the trails that provide sweeping views of the entire city. She is eager to take a long walk in Doctors' Garden Park. Then there is the villa that once belonged to another of her deceased uncles. Where would it be? Somewhere in the city or the suburbs— but where? A trip to the town hall most likely will help with that. Then she remembers that her mother often talked about Varna. Should they drive to that seaside town? She scratches that idea. They're not likely to find anything in Varna. Her parents spent vacations there, but why would any personal history be there? Anyway, it's clear across the country, east of Sofia, on the Black Sea. It was and still is the most popular vacation spot for city-dwellers. Sofia, where they are now, is in the west near Serbia. They will have to travel to where her father was born, Ruse, or Ruczuk, depending on how old you are and which language you speak. That city is northeast of Sofia on the shores of the Danube, directly across from the Romanian border. To the south of Sofia is Turkey and Greece where some of her story may lie. Her head is spinning with so much geography, but at least she is beginning to get her bearings. She is keen to understand what Bulgaria was like long before World War II and in the years after the war when the Communists changed it. Her mission is to find out where her ancestors lived and what they made of their lives. Mulling this over, she reminds herself that she is in a foreign city with a man she only recently met. Her sister would be shocked. It has been a surprising turn of fate. The trip was unplanned—but then she rarely makes plans at all, functioning more on instinct and circumstance, than organization. But she has run out of steam. She knows she must digest and explore everything, but acknowledges that right now she is hungry and exhausted.

Michael has been very kind and while they've been traveling together for hours, Beka still feels shy around him. She has learned very little about him and worries that she coerced him into joining her quest. Yet he is easy to be with and is proving to be a good companion who doesn't seem to require a lot of attention. He's very presentable and self-assured. It's nice too, that he is about two inches taller than she is. Why that is important she cannot say. She's been very self-absorbed and hasn't demonstrated much interest in him, but she is curious, only holding back because she senses she should not pry. Nonetheless it hasn't stopped her from wondering about him. What does he think about? Is he a Republican? She hopes not. Does he have a family somewhere? Did he, or does he have a wife? Children? All she knows is that he was brought up in England and went to the University here and did his graduate work at Oxford. He speaks Bulgarian fluently, and will know how to find his way around. That's probably what's most important. Exhausted by her thoughts, Beka decides it's best to stop thinking.

They find a few shops nearby where they make some purchases. The shopping goes quickly, neither of them particularly interested in being too selective. Dropping the bundles off at the apartment, they walk a short distance before finding a relatively nice-looking restaurant.

Beka is grateful to see familiar food on the menu written in both English and Bulgarian. In fact, the restaurant smells like her mother's kitchen. She knows exactly what she wants to order. The banitza looks different than her mother's and here it is spelled banitsa, but turns out to taste just the same. Made of filo dough, butter and cheese, it was always made during the holidays at home, but here it seems to be on the menu and eaten at any time of day. She orders a cold yogurt and cucumber soup with walnuts and decides to have some Bulgarian wine along with thick peasant bread and kashkaval, delighted to see it on the menu. It is a name she hasn't heard in years. This cheese was a staple in her mother's kitchen. Michael orders a glass of Rakija, a popular brandy made of various fermented fruit, and a Gyuvech, a slow-cooked stew containing beef, mushrooms, onions, and peppers with a heavy dose of paprika. While she has rarely prepared these dishes herself, she remembers them well. Finally relaxing in this cheerful restaurant, they notice that it is beginning to fill up with people and a band is setting up on the small stage at the back of the room. Before long, they are treated to music and a troupe of Kolo dancers in bright peasant costumes. They look at each other and smile with delight. A sense of warmth envelops her. It's like being covered in a feather duvet on a cold winter's night.

At morning's first light, Beka is wide awake. She walks to the window to make sure she hasn't been dreaming. The buildings across the street look residential and respectable. At the end of the street there is a yellow rococo six-story building. Instead of the building having a ninety-degree angle, it curves gently around the corner with balconies that wrap around the building. It reminds her of something her mother told her about the broad boulevards of Vienna and the buildings with rounded corners and balconies. That, she said, was a sign of prosperity. Beka reckons this must have been a prosperous neighborhood too.

Unpacking the coffee machine and the package of coffee they bought yesterday, she brews enough for a few cups, figuring Michael will want one when he wakes up. Entering the dining room through the French doors, she has her first strange sensation. The French doors begin to grow larger as though she is seeing them as a baby might see them when lying in a cradle. They rise above her. Startled at the mirage, she gasps. As the sensation passes and the image fades, she wonders, "Was I that baby?"

Fighting off jetlag, Beka wonders what to do with the day. Returning to the kitchen for a second cup of coffee, she meets Michael in the hallway. Always the one that is awake before anyone else, she is delighted to see that Michael is also an early riser. Being in tune might help make their time together easier and more productive.

Michael pours a cup of coffee, turning to Beka,

"Let's explore Sofia today and make arrangements to meet your cousin later in the week, or perhaps tomorrow."

Relieved that Michael is willing to serve as a guide and allow her the joy of exploring the city before diving into the research that brought them here, she enthusiastically agrees.

4

THE KEY

MICHAEL AND BEKA sit in one of the state-owned fast trains heading for Ruse. Modern, plain but relatively comfortable, it is the last evening train out of Sofia and expected to arrive in Ruse at two in the morning. Disappointed by the clean plastic interior of the train, Beka hoped it would be a somewhat threadbare, but still richly appointed luxury train—like the Orient Express. She always had an exaggerated romance with the 1930s, though it was an era of extreme excess contrasting with devastating poverty. The years of the depression eventually led to the rise of Hitler and the start of a world war that destroyed most of Europe and lasted for six years. But for her, the thirties are still a fascinating study in contrasts, and her mind easily skips over the dark times and focus on what she loved most about the flavor of that era. The Orient Express exemplified the thirties and appealed to her because of its lavish Art Deco style. From architecture, to poster-art, to the fashions of the day, Art Deco was the expression of the thirties. Adding to it was the sweet sound of big band music and though it came a bit later, film noir was a world she was attracted to. Plush, overstuffed, polished brass, etched-glass, fragile porcelain cups, bias-cut gowns, elongated silhouettes of pure silk. She was under the sway of the Hollywood version of that time. Dressing for dinner, men wearing hats and vests and carrying walking sticks. Women in furs, and belted dresses. There was a formality that no longer exists in the current trend for casual comforts. She wonders what the train looked like when her father traveled to Sofia from Ruse while courting her mother.

It hadn't exactly been an arranged marriage. Her mother was free to choose, but their families had gotten together hoping to make a match. Beka figures her parents were probably attracted to each other, otherwise the marriage would not have taken place. Still, her mother was young and sheltered by her overprotective mother and of an age when being married was expected. Sultana David Avraham sometimes hinted that her husband, Jacob, may not have been her first choice. Once while sitting at their kitchen table watching her mother make BÖreks, she would begin to reminisce. Rolling out one layer of paper-thin dough after another, painstakingly buttering each layer as she placed one on top of the other, she wistfully began to talk of another liaison that was cut short by her parents. But just as her mother's memories were becoming interesting, she would stop, check the plum dumplings boiling on the stove and not resume the conversation no matter how much Beka pleaded.

Though Sultana never once said anything disparaging about her mother, Zora, it was her older sister, Flor, that had taken on the job of raising her. Her mother had already raised three children, now almost adults, and wasn't inclined to be burdened by another, often calling Sultana a mistake—a comment Sultana took to heart, even as she tried to break free from the restrictions her mother placed on her. Consequently, there were things she never learned to do: like drive a car, or how to swim. Her mother's restrictions had not been dealt as punishment nor did she mean to be cruel, but rather it was an expression of Zora's guilt over the dereliction of her real motherly duties.

Her sister became Sultana's closest friend. They remained close, even after Flor, whom they were sure would remain a spinster, surprised everyone by announcing her intention to marry Benno Avraham, who oddly enough was a first cousin to Beka's father, Jacob. This meant that when they both married, the sisters would have the same last name.

When Sultana's father died, and all the David children were married, the family apartment became too large for her mother. Growing older, a diabetic and quite portly, Zora decided to move into the smaller first-floor apartment in the building she owned, situated on a beautiful square in the heart of Sofia. She asked Flor and Benno to take up residence in the family apartment she was vacating.

Flor's husband, Benno was known to be a practical joker. With his dark, round-rimmed glasses and bowler hat, he seemed by all appearances, a reserved figure, which is why it was surprising that he had such a silly sense of humor. One of his favorite routines was to dress up as a woman at unexpected times, convincing his mother-in-law, Zora, now nearly blind, that he was her old friend, Sarah, who often came to visit. He would sit in her parlor having tea, Zora never the wiser.

After the war, Flor and Benno moved to Istanbul and Flor's letters always assured Sultana that they were getting along and happy, until the day Benno, in his short-sightedness, accidentally fell to his death in an open elevator shaft.

Much of what Beka knows about her family never came directly from her parents, but rather from hearsay or the photo albums that fed her imagination. Often as a child, she would examine the early photos of her young parents, with detailed curiosity. Her mother was a young, beautiful and fashionable woman who had spirit and panache. Marriage, the War and her displacement seem to have subdued some of those attributes.

When her parents first married, they lived in another building owned by Sultana's parents. Aching to be an independent woman, she convinced Jacob to buy the apartment on Krakra Street, but before she could taste independence, her mother-in-law, Vivenza, known to the grandchildren as Vivachi, moved to Sofia from Ruse. Sultana would often describe her as a harsh, intimidating woman. But that wasn't the only thing she said about her mother-in-law.

"If she wasn't dismissing whatever I had to say, she was complaining about my cooking and how I kept the house. She couldn't understand why I grew so tall, saying it wasn't natural! When I first married your father, I was relieved that my in-laws lived in a distant city. When they moved to Sofia, my every move was closely inspected."

In the only photograph of Vivenza that Beka has, she looks like a stout compact woman with hair tightly pinned back, wearing a print silk dress down to her ankles with thick stockings and worn shoes poking out from under her skirt. Looking straight at the camera, holding a cup of coffee, she seems to be telling the camera to hurry up with this picture-taking. She has work to do!

—

Though they are traveling to Ruse to investigate her father's side of the family, Beka's thoughts seem to stay with her mother. She turns to Michael, wanting to share her thoughts, but seeing him read the newspaper with an intimidating concentration, she remains silent. He hasn't said very much of anything yet, and she wonders about that. Staring out at the night, she watches the streetlights come and go as they pass outside the train's window, illuminating the scenery for just a moment before growing dark again, like a light switch being turned on and off. Neglecting to bring anything to read, she yawns and soon falls asleep.

Gently being shaken awake, Beka hears Michael whisper,

"We are here, Beka, don't forget your bag."

Hastily, Beka retrieves her belongings and stumbles down the aisle, behind Michael, following him off the train. Before her, she sees an elegant railroad station, large and imposing. She is walking on marble floors and looks up to see the high ceilings and pillars rising to a balcony that encircles the entire hall. This is not the station her father would have used. This station was built later, sometime in the 1950s and much closer to the center of town. She pads after Michael, still groggy from sleep and the late hour, towards the street and a taxi stand. The cab ride to the hotel only takes a few minutes. They might have walked, though she is thankful they did not.

The plaque at the side of the main door of the hotel announces it was built in 1893. Entering, they see that Hotel Izvora has a lobby that is mixed with old elegance and contemporary bad taste. The floor has been covered with an asphalt white and blue tile that clashes with the rest of the interior. The furnishings are heavy and ornate. Michael interprets the conversation he is having with the man at the desk as Beka listens to the familiar sound of the hard-rolling language she heard growing up but never understood.

A set of stairs brings them to a very long hallway with Art Deco couches every few feet. Michael's room is next door to Beka's. He wishes her a goodnight and kisses her on the forehead.

"We can sleep in and then find our way to Municipality Hall after breakfast." Beka, too sleepy to respond to what seems only a friendly kiss, mumbles goodnight.

When she opens the door to her room, she is surprised at how large it is. The overdone interpretation of neo-classical furniture makes her laugh. The dark patterned wallpaper seems to want to suffocate the room. The windows are large and have elaborately draped silk curtains. This definitely isn't the Holiday Inn, and she estimates the room will only cost $30 per night.

—

Irritated by the attitude of the women they encounter at the Municipality Hall who all seem burdened and disinterested, Beka feels the immensity of her project and how it might drift towards nothing at all. They've spent the morning waiting for hours in this ugly building in a park with fountains and statuary, only to be sent from one office to another. Beka finds herself snapping at everyone—even Michael.

"We have looked for files for this family, Avraham, but there is nothing here."

Irritated Beka cries, "But there must be some tax records, something. They were here. They lived here for decades!"

"These offices," the lady states with stilted politeness, "do not have the kind of records you are looking for. Perhaps you should visit the town hall or the synagogues."

When they leave the building Beka suggests they separate and meet up at the hotel later in the afternoon. Michael does not disagree. He is not enjoying Beka's temper and is eager to reacquaint himself with the city. Beka, realizing that she has been on too short a fuse, knows she'd better calm down and not alienate Michael. Before they part, he suggests they might try the town hall tomorrow, as it is not far from the hotel.

Not really comfortable about trying to negotiate even simple things in this country where all the signs are printed in Cyrillic, Beka decides to walk in the direction she thinks will lead her to the Danube. From her map she knows it will be quite a long walk but doesn't want to attempt public transportation or a taxi, fearing she will not be understood and anyway, she hasn't yet figured out the monetary system.

Discovering, to her dismay, after walking for a few miles, that there is a highway between the river and where the street ends. She is relieved to find a bench. Her feet are burning from the long walk. She pulls out the map indicating the only real access to the river is near the Friendship Bridge that connects Ruse with Romania, and it is miles away. Ruse is much bigger than she imagined. It is not at all how she'd pictured this city. She was sure the part of town where her father grew up was rural and that the Danube was a romantic river, not a busy industrial lane. There is nothing rural about what she has seen of the city so far, and she has no idea where her father's childhood home is. Her objective today was to find that address and to see what she envisioned all her life—a grassy park leading to the banks of the Danube. But now it seems hopeless. She always imagined her adolescent father and his friends gathering at the river's edge, swimming fearlessly across the river to Romania. From where she sits, she reckons the river is about a mile and half wide. It looks like it has strong currents and a lot of large ship traffic. Swimming across must have been dangerous. What was he like as a teenager? She only knew him as a cautious man, but the few stories he told her, suggests he could be disobedient and reckless and that his deeds often cost him a scolding from his sharp-tongued mother.

Retracing her steps, Beka heads back to the hotel, tired, cranky and discouraged.

—

Leaving Beka on the steps of the Hall, Michael wanders aimlessly around the residential streets, stopping when he finds an open-air market. Strolling among the colorful stalls, he absentmindedly picks up items without much interest and then sets them back down and moves along.

Stopping at a stall, he spots a small leather pouch. The leather is old, cracked and discolored. It has a crude hook that serves as a lock that keeps its contents in place. Opening it, he sees to his surprise, pressed into the leather, the faded name *Avraham*. There is an antique key inside the pouch. Picking it up, he examines it and excitedly asks the woman seated behind the makeshift counter if she knows anything about the pouch. He wonders how old it might be? The woman takes it from him, looks up at him with an expression that Michael cannot decipher.

"Yes. This pouch is centuries old. Why, do you want it?"

"I think so. The name on the pouch intrigues me. I am visiting this city with a woman who has the same name."

"Well, let's see. I can sell it to you for one hundred and fifty levas."

Michael rummages through his pockets and tries to hand her the coins. She gestures to a small dish beside her. As he obediently drops the coins in the dish, he asks,

"So, do you know anything about this pouch?"

She counts the coins slowly and folds them into a cloth purse, wraps the pouch in brown paper and hands him the package. Michael notices that she is wearing rings on every one of her fingers. Her distinctive blue eyes seem to pierce through her softly wrinkled skin, making it difficult to determine her age.

"Yes, there is a story that goes with this pouch and the key. House keys, you may know, were often kept by the Jews, when they were chased out of Spain during the Inquisition, in the hope that they might return to their homes one day. This one has come down through the centuries along with its story. The key, so the story goes, belonged to Ledicia Serrano who arrived in Edirne Turkey in the year 1493, from Castile. When she became the wife of Isaiah Avraham, she had the pouch embossed with his name. It was one of the possessions that their oldest son inherited after the death of his parents. The son, Naftali, held on to it as did all the other members of the family, through many generations. Along with the pouch, the story is told of the Inquisition and Ledicia and Isaiah's life. It was a family tradition to tell the story to each generation. I can tell you the story if you like, as it was told to me."

Intrigued, Michael, completely astonished, sits down on the curb and listens. Smoothing out her skirt, she folds her jeweled hands on her lap and begins.

Castile, Spain
March, 1492

When Ledicia overhears her father's name mentioned by two men whispering behind the pillared walls of the temple, she becomes alarmed. She runs home to warn her father. At seventeen years of age, she is no stranger to the danger of being a Jew in Spain. The Catholic church has been determined to rid Spain of the Jews for some time.

Her father, Naftali Serrano, has been severely criticized for his work. His commentaries on Thomas Aquinas' interpretation of Aristotelian philosophy are considered blasphemous by the Church. Ledicia has already witnessed the hatred and brutality towards her people, and is fearful that the government, dictated by the Catholic Church, will label her father a heretic. Yet no one in her family can imagine the possibility that he might be killed or forced into exile as so many others have been.

Entering her home, a crumbling stone structure where her family lives in three crowded rooms, Ledicia hears her mother crying.

"They have taken him away." Holding her head in her hands she chants, "I knew it. I knew it, God help us."

Ledicia, overcome with fear, does not stop to comfort her mother or her two brothers, but runs out of the house without a word, crossing the courtyard, passing their small garden where they are allowed to grow vegetables. Once back on the street, she walks warily to the home of Rabbi Judah ben Joseph who has already heard of her father's abduction and insists that Ledicia and her family must prepare to leave the city. Her father will most likely be killed for his writings, and they are in danger. He hands her a sheet of paper with instructions that he hopes she will follow.

"I am preparing to leave Castile, and plan to go to Amsterdam. Spain is no longer safe for practicing Jews and hasn't been for years. The fact is that Jews are no longer welcome in most of Europe. Auto de Fe (acts of faith) are being practiced by the church. These trials are being conducted to determine the veracity of Jews who practice their religion which the Catholic Church

has decreed a heresy. The trials are a mockery, of course, and almost everyone who stands trial is imprisoned or worse. You must leave."

Returning home, Ledicia, is in conflict. She takes seriously what the Rabbi has said, but is unwilling to abandon her father, a man she loves and admires for his brilliance and his kindness to her. He has treated her as he would a son, adamantly believing that women should have the same rights as any man. Reading and writing should not only be the domain of men.

Huddled in the dimly-lit room with her family, they wait for news of Naftali, which does not come until the morning when they learn where he has been imprisoned. She immediately sets out to find her father. As she enters the courtyard of the prison she is turned away by the soldier on guard, even while he admires her thick dark hair and large blue eyes. He shouts sternly,

"You cannot enter. Go home!" Then looking around furtively, whispers,

"Leave as soon as you can. You are not safe here."

"Please sir. I am looking for my father."

The soldier whispers, 'They won't let you see him. I cannot help you."

Two days later the news they all dread arrives by messenger. They are given a formal letter with the government seal boldly stamped in red wax. Their mother's husband, their father, has been tried, found guilty and sentenced to death. They will not be allowed to see or bury him. The rumor is that he will be burned alive and his remains tossed into an open grave with other religious dissidents.

Hearing the news, Ledicia's mother collapses still holding the letter. Ledicia's brothers carry their mother to her bed and try to comfort her, but she will neither eat nor drink. Within three days she is dead, still clutching the letter, never again speaking another word.

—

The woman stops and clasps her hands.

"So, the story goes. The Alhambra Decree, known as the Spanish Inquisition was issued on the last day of March in 1492, by the Catholic Monarchs of Spain.

*"All practicing Jews are to leave the country
or convert to Catholicism."*

"Ledicia and her brothers find their way to Edirne, Turkey. There are no public records that detail this journey out of Spain, but it is known that the Ottomans sent ships to various ports to take Jews to their countries. What is believed is Ledicia and her two younger brothers traveled to Cape Finisterre in Galicia where they were transported to Turkey. It is also known that they survived the trip and that she lived in Turkey, producing children sired by the man she married, Isaiah ben Avraham."

"How, did you come to be in possession of this pouch and its history?" asked Michael.

The woman who at first seemed old, now looks less so. Fixing her blue eyes on Michael, she has a mysterious smile on her face. She smiles and sits straighter in her chair, but says nothing. He persists with another question.

"May I ask your name."

"Yes, you may ask, she says still smiling. My name is Madame Avraham, Rachael Avraham and I am here every nice day at noon.

Bombing of Sophia
Bombing of Sofia

5

MESSENGER FOR THE KING

MICHAEL, EXCITED BY his meeting with this mysterious woman, returns to the hotel hoping to find Beka there. He thinks he may have just uncovered the beginning of Beka's story. Disappointed that she has not returned, he leaves a message at the front desk and heads down to the tavern. Ordering an espresso, he looks over the notes he took a few days ago, while still in Sofia, when they spent an afternoon with Beka's cousin, Petya.

Sofia, Bulgaria
January 13, 2003

Petya greets Beka and Michael graciously, happy to finally meet a cousin he's only vaguely heard about. His mother, Irina, is the sister of Beka's father. Still a good-looking man at his advanced age, Petya is congenial, self-assured, and still embraces the fashion and attitude of a gentleman from another era. He was a teenager when the Second World War broke out and lived in Bulgaria during the Russian occupation.

Neither Michael nor Beka experienced the hardships of living in Bulgaria during and after the war. Michael's family left for Northampton, England a few years before the war and Beka's family emigrated to America after the war in Europe began.

The veranda of Petya's ancestral home has a wonderful view of the city. The weather is chilly but pleasant enough to sit outside. He fills their glasses with wine even before they are completely empty and places a large round of hard cheese and a course peasant bread before them. Settling back in his chair, he begins to recollect stories from his youth in a way that suggests he has told them many times.

Sofia, Bulgaria
March 10, 1944

At almost fourteen, Petya is beginning to think a lot about girls and is oddly fascinated by guns. He acquires one secretly which he has hidden in his bedroom in their apartment in Sofia. This clandestine acquisition will cause some panic a few years later, when, just as the war is coming to an end, the Russians search their home. Only by minutes is Petya and his father able to dispose of it before the Russians find it.

Not paying much attention to what is going on in his country or the world, he is mostly focused on boyish concerns. So, when he hears planes flying overhead, he doesn't think much about them. While he's aware that there is a war going on, he hasn't been touched by it. He assumes the planes are on the way to the oil fields of Romania and so he continues to read his mystery novel. All-of-a-sudden the sky over Sofia is ablaze. He runs out into the garden to see that the night sky is as bright as day. Though he is frightened, he can't tear himself away. By morning they learn the center of Sofia was bombed by the allies and there are many civilian casualties and considerable damage to buildings.

At the same time, in America, Beka and Riva are placed in an orphanage while their parents look for work and a place to live. The orphanage, called 'The Home,' is not a bad place. They enjoy the big old-fashioned house with many rooms and the large winding staircase that the children run up and down all day long. There are children of all ages to play with, but because Beka is so young, she is often left out of the games the other children play. Beka misses her parents and can only see them through the screened-in porch on visiting Saturdays because they are often quarantined due to outbreaks of Scarlet Fever. A few months later Beka and her family are finally settling into their new apartment in Brookline, Massachusetts. Reva, and particularly Beka, are very happy to be back with their parents after months apart.

The first morning they are in their new apartment, the war still in progress, Beka's mother receives a letter from her sister Flor, writing to give them the news their mother has passed away. Unable to obtain insulin that controlled her diabetes she fell into a coma and never recovered. Huddled in their room, Beka and her sister listen to their mother's uncontrollable sobs, shivering with fear and a sadness of their own.

After dinner, they hear sirens; a sound that is heard frequently, and words like blackout and air raids are on everyone's lips. Curtains are drawn. They must shelter inside their apartment. Their neighbor, an air raid warden, knocks on all the doors to make sure orders are being followed. Lights out and blinds drawn. When the all-clear siren blasts, there is a collective sigh of relief.

Michael's family, living in Northampton are fortunate not to experience the war directly nor the kind of fear that grips London and other areas of England that are being targeted for destruction by the Germans.

Northampton is a very quiet place and life remains relatively normal. National rationing has been initiated, so there is a shortage of foods and goods.

A single bomb fell in the Duston area early in the war. That is as close as the Luftwaffe has come to bombing the town. The bomb tore up dozens of graves and shattered the windows in nearby houses, but no one was hurt. There is an assumption that the bombs that were dropped that day, were left over from a raid further west, and, most likely, the Germans disposed of them randomly. No one ever discovered exactly what happened. Otherwise, it has remained so quiet that some of the people in the town give up going to the shelter when the air raid sirens wail.

The town folk sometimes hear and see enemy planes overhead as they head to and from the industrial West Midlands, but for some reason the Luftwaffe ignores their town. It is the people on fire-watch duty, however, who never forget the light in the night sky that marked the burning of Coventry. While the town remains mindful and does take certain precautions, Michael continues to go school, his father, the local physician, continues to see patients, and his mother teaches piano lessons to the local children.

In Sofia, people are fleeing the capital. The government and the ministries evacuate their offices. It becomes increasingly difficult to get supplies of any kind. Petya's father understands the gravity of the situation having been part of the failed negotiations to get Bulgaria out of the Axis treaty, and the reason the Americans just bombed parts of the City. He decides to move the family to Istanbul which has not entered the war. They leave Petya's grandmother behind, along with a few other families who have taken refuge in their villa.

Petya puts his glass down.

"Did you know, Beka, that my father, your uncle, was involved in very serious political negotiations between Bulgaria, the Turks and the Americans?"

"No, I had no idea. I mean, how was he involved, and with whom?"

"Please have some cheese, you will like it. It's made at a local farm." Offering both Michael and Beka the platter of the hard-crusted bread and cheese, Petya continues his story which seems to be hard-wired to his memory.

"I need to go back to August of 1943. At that time, it was becoming clear that Germany might lose the war. King Boris was to meet with Hitler at his East Prussia headquarters. Prior to that meeting, King Boris called my father and asked for a meeting. Prime Minister, Boghan Filov, joined them. Unlike King Boris, the Prime Minister was sympathetic to Germany. The King asked my father to set up a meeting in Istanbul with a Turkish representative connected to the allies. The focus of the meeting was to explore the conditions by which Bulgaria would separate from their pact with the Germany.

Michael interrupts.

"Beka, you should understand why Bulgaria joined the Axis. Initially, the Bulgarians wanted to remain neutral. However, when faced with the threat of a German invasion, and the promise of regaining the Thrace territory they had lost to the Greeks in another altercation, the government decided to join the Tripartite Pact. Simply defined, it was a military alliance between Germany, Italy, and Japan along with other countries like Romania, Hungary, Yugoslavia etc. Except for a few intellectuals who saw Hitler for what he was, there wasn't much popular opposition for joining the pact at the time." Michael looked over at Petya.

"I'm sorry Petya, please continue, I thought she should understand this."

"Yes, of course." Clearing his throat, Petya continues.

"My father was not a diplomat nor a politician, but he often led missions abroad on behalf of the government. He had previously negotiated with Turkey on many occasions, primarily to supply Turkish cotton to the Bulgarian textile industry. His trips to Istanbul would, therefore, not arouse the suspicions of the Gestapo. At that meeting, my father was informed by the Americans, that the Allies placed great importance on the Bulgarian government to take immediate   steps to separate from the pact.

Beka is hurriedly writing down notes. She wants to ask questions, but does not want to interrupt the flow of the story. Petya takes a few long pulls on his pipe and continues.

"And those steps would likely have been taken, except that a few days after King Boris returned from his meeting with Hitler, he became very ill and died. The cause of his death still remains a mystery. Many people believe he was poisoned by Hitler, but the official cause of death is said to be a heart attack. His death caused confusion and ultimately a stalemate, so the separation never occurred, even though most of the ruling circles and a large portion of the patriotic Bulgarian citizenry felt very strongly that Bulgaria needed to separate from Germany."

"Whether it was because of Prime Minister Filov's allegiance to Germany, or the death of the King, no one can say for certain. It was, however, the result of this failure that led the Americans to begin bombing Sofia. By the middle of August, the Soviet army stationed itself at the northern border of Bulgaria, and within a few days Russia declared war on Bulgaria and crossed over into Bulgarian territory. The entire Bulgarian government resigned, and the country was taken over by the communist-dominated Popular Front."

Petya stops long enough to take a bite of cheese. Michael looks over at Beka, who sits motionless. This is probably as close as she's come to knowing anything about Bulgaria's involvement in the Second World War. She is amazed that an uncle of hers played a small role in that history.

Not yet tired, Petya is more than willing to continue.

"I loved living in Istanbul. My sister and I roamed about the city's beautiful shrines and broad city walks. Unhappily, my father got word that he had been placed on a military reserve list and we were forced to return to Bulgaria. That was the beginning of what would be a very difficult time for my family.

Between Istanbul and Bulgaria
November, 1944

Arriving at the Bulgarian border, Petya and his family are stopped by Turkish soldiers and relieved of their identity cards. Forced to wait for hours in the driving rain, they are finally allowed to board the train to Sofia where they are met by Russian soldiers and their identity cards returned. Once at home, two men are waiting for them and demand their identity cards again, and this time, they arrest Petya's father without any explanation.

Petya follows his mother and sister into the Villa, too confused to react to what just happened. They discover the ground floor of their home has been appropriated by General Walter Oxley, head of the British mission in Bulgaria. The entire downstairs has been rearranged into a canteen for the guards of the general. Their home has been taken without permission, and they are stripped of their rights. Petya resents the soldiers using the family's furniture and their home as if it was theirs. At this point in the war, Germany is losing badly, and Bulgaria's statement of neutrality is not accepted, so the country is now under the thumb of the Allies, which includes Great Britain, the USA, and Russia. Unfortunately, Russia gains far more political influence over Bulgaria than the other two countries as the Bulgarians feared.

Petya, his sister Maria, and their mother are assigned to the second floor of their own house and forbidden to use the ground floor. They realize that they are considered the enemy and are completely unprepared for how their lives will change. His father is held at the Directorate of the Police, in Sofia, where all the leading politicians and people in public life are in custody and classified as Enemies-of-the-People. A "People's Court " is being assembled to decide their fate. Petya is terrified that his father will be executed.

Rumors are everywhere. Wherever they go, there are stories whispered about arrests and the vicious, revengeful acts the Russians are committing. Petya learns that the prisoners are barely given anything to eat. The families are allowed to bring parcels of food to the prisoners once a week. Russian guards often keep the members of the family waiting in line for hours, then ransack their parcels, taking what they want for themselves.

Petya is assigned to bring food parcels to his father. A few weeks after his father's arrest, he takes the parcel of food his mother packed carefully, to the police station. When he arrives, he is told his father is not on the list. The guards don't know where he is or won't tell. Terrified, the family spends the next month fearing the worst. Word finally comes that Gregor is in a labor and re-education camp where he will spend the next seven months.

Shortly after learning where he has been taken, but before there is any time to feel any relief, several policemen brandishing Kalashnikov rifles wake them up in the middle of the night.

"Pack your bags, take warm clothes, something to eat, blankets and wait outside."

Petya's mother stoically gathers their things together, comforting her daughter, trying to convince her children that they we will be alright. Their grandmother is allowed to stay in the villa, but all the rooms are locked, except her bedroom, bathroom, and kitchen.

Waiting in the cold night air, they have no idea where they are being sent. It is a full hour before an old police van shows up. They are hurried into the van without a word spoken. The frost is caked on the wooden benches and *the cold seeps into their bones. It seems like hours before the van stops. Forced out of the van they see they are in front of a half-bombed-out building where women and children have been deposited. Petya notices that there are no men in the crowd. Throughout the night more frightened women and children arrive. In the morning they are loaded into livestock railroad cars. In the darkness of the cars, they spread out blankets for the younger children. Hours later the train stops at a small station in Northern Bulgaria called Isperich.*

Eventually they learn why all these people have been brought here. They are all related to someone who has been jailed and condemned as an enemy-of-the people, in the large show trials. The objective by the Russians is to get their relatives out of the city to avoid the families gathering together in protest. Learning this, Irina successfully gets her daughter released, persuading the guards that she is too young to pose a threat. Maria, is sent back to Sofia where she will be taken care of by an uncle and eventually sent to live in Italy for safety.

In Isperich, the mayor, a gloomy young man, stands in front of the large gathering. He seems confused about what he is being asked to do. Expressionless, he rattles off a written statement about what is to become of them.

"You will reside in the house of a local farmer and pay him rent. You may not talk to any of the village residents nor leave this village, and you will report to the community house three times a day."

The mayor never once looks up from the paper he is reading from. After he shouts these instructions, the farmer who drives them to a whitewashed farmhouse, isn't very talkative, but the peasant family they are assigned to seem sympathetic. The initial distrust on the part of the villagers eventually dissipates and life eases up considerably. The peasants' instinct to laugh, drink and sing, and their already hardening distrust of the government takes over any requirement to be obedient. Consequently, they do not take their job of harboring their guests seriously or reporting their behavior. Irina is frantic with worry about her husband and her daughter. To avoid thinking too much, she works doubly hard around the farm, which pleases her landlords, while Petya spends most of the four months of their stay in the village library.

Meanwhile, death sentences are being carried out. The newspapers print long lists of the condemned. Each time they open the paper, they are afraid they will discover Gregor's name on the list. By April, the show trials come to an end and Gregor's name still has not appeared. Relieved, they are allowed to go home. Their first internment has come to a peaceful end, but it will not be the last hurdle they will jump.

Petya takes his pipe and begins tinkering with it.

Beka can see that Petya is still affected by the events he has lived through and she feels humbled and genuinely grateful that her parents emigrated to America in the early days of the war and were not exposed to the war or its aftermath. It is clear to her now that she's been completely oblivious to what was going on and that even when the war came to an end, the Bulgarian people were still obliged to contend with the harsh rules imposed by a new Communist government.

She wants to learn more about the entire post-war period in Bulgaria, but it is growing late. They leave Petya sitting on the patio under a darkening sky, puffing thoughtfully on his pipe, and promise to return soon. Michael is excited that he is learning more about life behind the Iron Curtain from one who lived through it. Beka, on the other hand, is deeply affected now that she knows what some of her family went through during the war. What else will she learn? She is very quiet on the ride back to the hotel.

—

Michael looks up from his notebook in time to see Beka standing at the entrance of the tavern. Glancing over the room, she sees him and waves as she walks towards his table. For the first time, he notices how lightly she walks. Despite the lines on her face and her shoulders that sometimes bend forward, her face is always lively. She can look almost regal at times, even in blue jeans. But as she approaches Michael's table, he sees how tired she looks.

"Damn, I'm exhausted!" She says as she sinks noisily into the empty chair.

"What are you drinking, Michael? Coffee? Isn't it five o'clock yet? I think I need something stronger!" She signals the waiter and asks for a Rakia, then looks at Michael to confirm that she ordered it correctly. He smiles and nods. She gracelessly stretches out her legs.

"I think I've walked the entire width of Ruse. I can't feel my feet! What about you, what have you been up to?"

Michael opens his briefcase and takes out the leather pouch he purchased earlier, places it on the table and pushes it towards Beka, "Have a look!"

Tzar Shishman St. Ruse, Bulgaria

6

THE NEXT DAY

T HE HULKING SIZE and aggressive gracelessness of the City Hall resembles a battleship. Constructed during the Soviet era, it is representative of the Communist ideology imposed on the entire country:
The government's way of insinuating the 'State' on the people. Intimi-
dated by its size, Beka takes a deep breath as they enter. This time when
she enquires about her father's family, Beka is elated to find there is
a record showing that Joseph Avraham, her paternal grandfather and
Vivenza (Vivachi) Avraham, her grandmother, lived on Tzar Shishman
Street in Ruse, through the early 1930s.

Hailing a cab, they drive along Port Street where they see a broad
walkway parallel to the river, reassuring Beka that it is possible to access
the more peaceful river from here, validating her father's story that he
and his friends used to swim across to Romania.

The taxi stops in front of a neglected building. It resembles an elderly person wrapped in thread-worn clothing hiding the bones of a once sturdy structure. Walking through the unhinged entry gate, almost hidden in a thicket of overgrowth, they walk up the cracked stone pathway to the front door. There are vines growing up and inside the stucco walls. Patches of brick are visible where the stucco has fallen off. Brambles and tall weeds surround the structure. The second floor of the house juts out a few feet further than the first floor. Michael points out that is a common feature seen in Balkan architecture. Beka turns to Michael,

"This building must have been abandoned for years".

Curiously the door is not locked. Wondering whether the door will fall off its hinges, Beka turns the latch gingerly. The door is stuck, then creaks but remains intact.

Holding her breath, Beka whispers. "So, this was my father's childhood home!"

Walking into the anteroom, they step on the moss-covered tile floor. There is a wooden bench built against the wall which for some reason makes Beka want to weep.

"My father probably took off his shoes and hung up his jacket right here."

Michael nods. "It was common practice to remove your shoes before entering the house. Often there were slippers kept right here for guests."

Entering the main room, the moldy air makes her sneeze. She notices the decaying remnants of a few pieces of furniture. They almost seem to be embarrassed by their current state of abandonment. The gloomy presence of the exterior of the building is mitigated by sun streaming through the once-beautiful ornate windows that take up an entire wall at the side of the room. Underneath the window there is a built-in wooden bench the full length of the wall, covered in a faded torn fabric. Michael points to the banquette,

"That's another typical Bulgarian furnishing. You'll see these everywhere."

Shredded curtains cling to the windows. A faded mural takes up the opposite wall that leads to a hallway. At the far corner of the room, a curved stucco-covered fireplace still has firewood in the side cubby and ash in the firebox.

Michael looks around, curious to see what the mural depicts, but cannot make anything of it. Turning to Beka he continues his instructional conversation, while Beka, barely listening, stands in the middle of the room mesmerized.

"It was not uncommon for farm animals to be kept on the ground floor of the house, while the family lived on the second floor. Likely this house was remodeled so that this floor could accommodate a growing family."

Because the windows are boarded up in the other rooms, it's too dark to see what's in them. Luckily, they remembered to bring a flashlight. But these rooms are bare. One room looks like it was probably a dining room as a door at the far end leads to the kitchen which is at the very back of the house.

Through the door, Beka can see the entire kitchen as the windows are not boarded up. Walking over to the cast iron sink, she suddenly feels the spirit of her grandmother Vivenza. She can almost hear her harping and scolding her children as well as her husband. Beka visualizes her stocky volatile grandmother standing in the doorway, hands on hips, her shrill voice reverberating throughout the house. Though she never knew her and more than eighty years have gone by, Beka feels her overbearing personality still clinging to this room.

September 9, 1918
Tzar Shishman 17, Ruschuk (Ruse), Bulgaria

Joseph Avraham, arms full, pushes open the door of the kitchen with his knee and lays the parcels on the kitchen table. He has concluded his errands and looks forward to sitting down with a cup of tea, his pipe and the bible. Vivenza, peeling potatoes at the sink doesn't look up. Without greeting him, she walks over to the table and unwraps the parcels. First taking a deep breath, she then screams at Joseph in a fury.

"You bought the wrong cut of lamb!" She picks it up and hurls it out the window.

Joseph shakes his head in disgust, goes out and retrieves the meat, brushes it off and puts it back on the table. He pours himself a cup of tea without looking at her.

"Well, my dear, you'll just have to fetch what you want yourself, and if you think money grows on trees, please be sure to tell me where they are!" Shaking his head, he walks away. He has been ignoring his wife's temper for years, no longer sensitive to her outbursts, particularly so today. He has no intention of losing his temper now or his good mood. Not when he expects a visit from his oldest daughter and his grandchildren later in the day.

Yesterday they received an unexpected note from Lize, letting them know she would be arriving in the early evening with her children, though she makes no mention of whether her husband will be accompanying them. Joseph hasn't seen his daughter since her marriage to Isak, nor has he seen his three young grandchildren, Hugo, Gina and Benjamin.

Lately, Joseph feels his house has become much too quiet, except for his wife's frequent bellows. His oldest son Asher left to join the Greek army wanting to get his military duty over with. His other son, Charlo is away at university, and his youngest daughter Irina recently eloped with Gregor, a Bulgarian gentile. Lize, his oldest daughter lives in Vienna. Only Jacob, the youngest is still at home. Joseph whose greatest joy had always been his role as the patriarch of the large family, hasn't grown accustomed to the lack of busy noise and the vibrant energy his family provided.

Joseph hears his sixteen-year-old son, Jacob (the boy that will one day become Beka's father) being roundly scolded for injuring himself while he and his friends were climbing the fence at the end of the road. Running into the house, bleeding badly he asked his mother to help him.

"You have been told time and again not to climb that fence. Look you have torn your good pants. Go to the clinic immediately and have them take care of your bruises."

Jacob's arm is throbbing and the gash on his knee is bleeding into his torn trousers. The clinic is a mile away. Leaving the house in tears, he curses his mother as he walks down the road towards the clinic. Joseph runs after him and accompanies him the rest of the way.

Oddly enough, Jacob is his mother's favorite son, even though she never shows it; but then Vivenza doesn't believe in showing affection or pampering anyone. Days after that incident, Jacob is sitting on the kitchen steps while his mother is hanging up laundry, vociferously complaining about her neighbors.

"They never clean the latrine or replace the paper. They always leave it to others."

Jacob, painfully aware of how disagreeable his mother can be, still loves her and frequently tries to tease her out of her dark moods. Sitting on the back steps whittling, as he often does, he looks up and calls to her.

"Mother! You're such a grouch and you speak like a peasant. Maybe you 'should better' stick to Ladino," mimicking her broken Bulgarian. This time his teasing has the opposite effect. "Listen, Ti neshtastno dete (You, miserable kid), it's good enough." She picks up her laundry basket and on the way into the house, slaps him.

He often teases her about her accent. She speaks Ladino (or Judeo-Spanish) the historic language of most Spanish Jews. It is really her main language rather than the language of the country she was born in. But she never had much schooling. Normally, Vivenza tolerates, even enjoys, Jacob's teasing though she feigns annoyance. He is the only one in the family that can make her laugh, and she loves him for it, though is slow to admit it.

Joseph loves all his children, but he can't help being particularly fond of Lize, probably because she was the first-born and always considered the most beautiful. He waits patiently for the hour of her arrival, but when she doesn't show up as expected he begins to worry. Vivenza, on the other hand is annoyed with the change in schedule. Any departure from what is expected throws her into a bad mood. She covers the dinner she prepared and goes to bed. Joseph stays up anxiously waiting for his daughter and grandchildren to arrive. When they do it is after midnight.

"I missed the early train and had to wait for hours for the last one." She gives her father a brief hug and ushers the children upstairs to get them ready for bed.

It takes another half hour to get the children quiet enough to go to sleep. Joseph is still sitting where she left him. She comes down the stairs, and without a word, slumps wearily into a chair next to her father and stares into the fire which is the only light in the room. Quiet tears begin to stream down her face. She is exhausted and hardly able to speak, even as Joseph implores her.

"What is it? What is the matter?" Joseph asks with alarm.

How does one explain that life has just taken an unimaginable turn? Guilt, fear, anger and grief are crushing Lize. It makes it hard to speak. She still has not told anyone. Turning to her father she tries to pronounce the words carefully without bursting into a torrent of tears

"My husband, Isak, is gone. He died three days ago."

—

Isak is a man who has always been strongly influenced by certain political beliefs. Recently he's been made head of the military wing of the Bulgarian partisans. He joined the group after the October Revolution. Though they live in Vienna, his business and his affiliations remain in Ruschuk. His own station in life is comfortable, but it does not prevent him from having deep sympathies for the Bolshevik's commitment to the teachings of Karl Marx—and the belief that the working class must liberate themselves from the economic and political control of the ruling class.

When the Bolsheviks kill Czar Nicholas and the entire Romanoff family, they steal some of the crown jewels. As a small but determined group of revolutionaries—they have very little money to buy arms to protect themselves and conduct their mission. Now in possession of these jewels, they ask Isak to travel to Berlin to sell them. He is their logical choice, because he, amongst all of them, travel frequently and, therefore, will not arouse suspicion. To doubly-secure his mission, Izak takes his young son with him and hides the jewels in his diaper. In later years, Benjamin will be kidded by the family. Benno, they will say, you can claim to have once peed on the infamous Romanoff jewels!

Belying his profitable business, a loving family, and an active commitment to a political cause that he deeply believes in, Isak cannot defeat the unexpected spells of depression that grip him at times. He has fought off these excruciatingly painful attacks by using every possible cure; healing waters, bathes, retreats, exercise and even a change of diet. These modalities seem to have worked, but he has never understood why he is victim to these bouts of anxiety and depression or why they leave him just as mysteriously. Not having had an attack for many years, he believes he has finally been cured.

Finishing his breakfast, he looks forward to going to work. He kisses his wife and children goodbye, and runs down the street to catch the tram.

Suddenly he begins to panic and becomes overwhelmed with feelings of despair. His body grows rigid and sweat begins to roll off his forehead. A paralyzing anxiety grips him. Barely able to reach his office, he tells the receptionist she can take the day off, as he cannot be disturbed. He locks the door behind himself, takes a bottle of schnapps from his desk drawer, pours out a glass, then another, until the bottle is empty. Staggering, he paces the floor of his office. From time to time, he lies down on the divan trying to fall asleep–but cannot. He is wide awake, choking as if he cannot breathe, feeling like he is teetering at the edge of a demon pit. The hours go by without relief. The sky darkens as the day turns into night and he knows he cannot go home. He can't endure another attack like this. Shaking, he empties the contents of his pockets, takes off his wedding ring and lays it on the desk but keeps the engraved pocket watch that Lize gave him on his last birthday. Locking his office door, he walks the half mile to the railroad station. As a train approaches, he begins to pray. His mind grows silent. The train's whistle shrieks in his ears and a wind begins to rise. Closing his eyes, he throws himself in front of the train.

—

Isak, a father of three, the husband of her Aunt Lize, and the uncle Beka will never know, died that day. Beka snaps out of her trance. She stares out of the window in front of the sink. Realizing where she is, she looks around for Michael, who has been calling to her.

"Up here Beka. You should see this old structure! Beka, still affected by whatever it was she witnessed, isn't able to respond. Michael continues to talk, not noticing Beka's changed mood.

Michael is standing at the head of the stairs looking out of a small window. "That's a latrine and from its location, it looks like it served those other two houses that share the same backyard." "Yes, I think that's right. It was shared with three other families." Beka wonders how she know this. She must have heard her father talk about it. Or maybe her sister mentioned it. Her sister always knew more about the family than she ever did.

"Y'know Michael, when I grew up in New York City, we had one small bathroom in our apartment which was shared by four people. Sometimes five when we had a boarder. Today that seems unthinkable.

But having a bathroom of one's own, must have been a luxury for my father."

"Interesting that my grandmother was able to tolerate that miserable latrine, but when she moved to an apartment in Sofia, with much better amenities, Vivenza apparently still found every reason to complain. She died before I was born so I will never know if I'd have been fond of her, or whether I would have disliked and feared her in the same way my mother and my aunts did."

Beka looks out at the backyard, remembering her father.

"You know, in spite of who she was, I recall on the rare occasions my father spoke of her, he would recount the day he stood by her bedside and watched over her, sick with pneumonia. She died in his presence. Whenever he recalled that moment, he always began to cry. It is really the only time I ever saw him cry."

It's already past noon and time for lunch. Beka has a hard time leaving this house, but they have plans to meet Rachael later in the day. Before leaving the area, they take a walk through the neighborhood and along the broad walkway skirting the river. Beka wonders if her father, seeing another country just across the river developed the restlessness she often observed in him.

"The war sent the family in many different directions. Before then, they had lived here for centuries." Beka turns to Michael as they hail a cab.

"Families were much larger then. They have grown smaller and smaller. Think about it. My father was one of five siblings: my mother one of four. I have one sister; my son is an only child and will likely have none. It's so different now."

7

LEAVING CASTILE

THE SUN IS already low in the sky when Michael and Beka reach the market where he first encountered Rachael. He wonders if she will still be there. If it were not for the leather pouch in his pocket, he is not sure if he didn't just imagine their encounter. When they turn the corner, she is there, just as she had been the day before.

"Hello, Madame Avraham. Michael extends his hand which Madame acknowledges with a slight bow of her head. "I would like you to meet my friend, Beka."

Smiling, Beka starts to extend her hand towards Madame but recalls the minor rebuff Rachael gave to Michael and slides her hand back into her coat pocket and simply nods.

Michael noticing the woman's reticence, clears his throat.

"Beka's last name is also Avraham."

Madame looks at Beka. It is impossible to know whether she is smiling or frowning.

"We are intrigued by the pouch I bought yesterday, and its story. Would it be possible to meet with you sometime this evening? Perhaps you would let us take you to dinner? We would love to do that."

While Michael is speaking to Madame in Bulgarian, Beka studies the woman's face. It is curiously familiar. There is something in the woman's eyes, a cloudy blue, that Beka is drawn to.

Madame looks at Michael first, then turns her gaze toward Beka, studying her for what seems a very long time. Pulling a card from beneath her shawl, she hands it to Michael.

"Come to my house instead. Be there at nine."

—

The address on the card indicates that Madame lives in the old town. It is still a lovely neighborhood, with broad walking streets, small shops and outdoor cafes. The European and Ottoman-inspired buildings are no more than four stories high. Madame lives in an ornate well-kept building painted bright yellow. There is a bookstore on the ground level. The front door is painted red. They walk up four very long, steep flights of stairs to reach her apartment, which is at the very top of the building.

Michael looks around at the narrowing landing and a door that seems to lead outside.

"I'm pretty sure this floor was originally the attic."

He takes Beka's hand and helps her up the final steps. She is trying to catch her breath.

"She does this every day? Beka gasps. "God bless her."

Greeting them at the door, Rachael is not wearing her large shawl. Without it she appears much younger than she did earlier in the day. Beka notices with some surprise, she has a dancer's walk and very lively gestures. Now without her head-covering, Beka sees that her hair is snowy white, combed back severely and gathered in a bun. Beka wonders if she stopped dying her own hair, would it turn as white as hers. Wearing a long woolen black dress cut on a bias, one can see clearly what wasn't evident before. Rachael is not very tall, and has a trim figure.

The main room seems to serve as both dining room and parlor. A small kitchen is in the rear. Madame gestures to a table, "Please have a seat."

Speaking to her in Bulgarian, Michael asks if she knows English. Rachael smiles broadly.

"Yes, I do. I also speak German and some French. Which language would you prefer I speak?"

Michael suggests English. Beka is delighted.

Rachael moves gracefully towards the kitchen. "Tea or wine? Bulgarian wine is not bad at all."

Madame is presenting an entirely different picture of herself. Now she seems so much younger. Almost elegant and seemingly worldly.

"Yes, wine please," Beka chimes in, relieved that she will be able to participate in the conversation.

As Madame Avraham pours the wine, Beka notices the rings on all the fingers of her hands,

"Oh my, your rings? You have so many. They are beautiful."

Madame, puts the decanter down and stares at her hands.

"Each of these rings was given to me by different people I cared about and at different times, so," she shrugs, "why not wear them all rather than have them collect dust in a box?"

This is the first time she has spoken directly to Beka. This makes Beka feel more relaxed. "There is a lot of history on your fingers." Madame, nods in acknowledgment and continues to pour the wine without further explanation.

Wanting to remain part of the conversation Beka decides to begin by inserting something personal.

"As you know, my name is Avraham too. I'm here to learn what I can about my family. We were both wondering, Michael and I, if you might be part of my family and if that pouch holds some significance, perhaps the beginnings of my family's history…or yours, or both."

When she gets no response, Beka continues to ramble on.

"I can't help wondering why you were selling the pouch? I mean, is it a family heirloom?"

Madame sits down, looks at Beka, slowly sipping her wine.

"It is my dear. I have other small treasures. I hoped by putting this one on display, I would attract someone's attention."

"Really?" Beka is surprised by her answer.

"What I mean is that I wondered if I put it out, someone might come along who knows more than I do about my family and the family I married into."

She puts down her glass. "I should start by tell you a few things about myself." Michael sits down at the table next to Madame, eager to hear what she has to say.

"I was born in Vienna, but when I was quite small, my family moved to Bulgaria, as did my husband's family, but his family eventually returned to Austria, so he was raised in Vienna only leaving when the war began. We both lost family during the war. Those that stayed in

Vienna were killed in the camps. But that, of course, is another horrific tale." Rachael pauses for a moment before continuing her monologue.

"My husband gave me the pouch among other things, and told me the story of Ledicia, just before he died, fifteen years ago." Settling back in her chair Madame continues. "I told Michael some of that story, the other day. So now if you like, I will continue, as it was told to me."

Both Beka and Michael say in unison, "Yes, please."

Castile, Spain, 16 Cheshvan 5252
March,1492

Unraveling the hair from the braided bun her mother always wore, Ledicia realizes she has never seen her mother's hair fully let down. It is softer and much longer than she imagined. The white strands shine brightly as though expressing delight at being set free. Tears come quickly but she stops them, unwilling to allow herself the luxury of grief. One thought that gives her comfort, is now her mother and father's spirit will be together. She is heartbroken that her father's body was not buried as he would have wished, prepared properly for burial according to Jewish law. Instead, he was burned alive and carelessly disposed of. She is convinced that his spirit will, despite this debasement, be swiftly allowed into heaven where their mother surely is.

With heavy shears she begins to cut her mother's hair. Though her mother lies silent in death, her hair seems very much alive. It takes Ledicia a moment before she dares to cut it off. There is something cruel about robbing her mother of her beautiful crown. But it is the only treasure she and her brothers own. That and her father's gold watch, which he, in a moment of clarity, took off before being led out of the house and to his death. The money she will receive for these two precious items will allow Ledicia and her brothers to escape the city and the inquisition's decree.

Preparing for their journey, Ledicia instructs her brothers to put on two sets of clothing which she does as well. She fills a leather bota with water and places a blanket, a knife, some cheese and a loaf of bread in a leather satchel. Almost forgetting, she finds the leather pouch that contains the key to their front door and puts it into the satchel. Maybe they will be able to return home someday. Finding the book her father just completed, the one she helped scribe, she wraps it in a tunic, and places it at the bottom of the satchel. Her father spent many of his days teaching his children how to read and write and made no exception when it came to his daughter.

Traveling for days in the back of a cart, heading for Lisbon, they are crowded in with several other families. They hope to find a ship that will take them to Edirne, Turkey. It is cold and the road is studded with rocks. They have very little room to move and the stench that has begun to permeate around them, mixed with the deadly silence of the other passengers, has worn down their spirits. They have been living in fear and a sadness that has no end. But with the generosity of some country folk who are driving them, and the words of the rabbi who gave them careful instructions, they hope by traveling east to Turkey they will find a better life.

Edirne, Turkey
June, 1492

Entering Edirne, after months of hardship, they arrive at a Sephardic Synagogue. All three are cold, half-starved and dirty. Ledicia sits on the floor and leans against the wall in the sanctuary next to her brothers. Shivering even though it is quite warm, they are thankful that they have been kept alive and have reached a place of safety. Exhausted and still heartbroken, they are fed, bathed and given clean clothes and allowed to rest.

It takes only a few days before they are fully recovered. They are young and strong and eventually well enough to be assigned places where they can live and work. The brothers are sent to a farm where they will work for their keep and receive a small stipend. Ledicia, unhappy to be separated from her brothers, is placed in the home of the merchant, Efron Hazan, where she is to perform household duties. Almost eighteen, Ledicia, has begun to flower into a strong-willed, lovely but sullen young woman. Her beautiful dark hair is covered with a rough cotton scarf, which she binds tightly over her forehead so that her light eyes are even more striking. She has become quiet and distrustful. Though she is separated from her brothers, she is thankful that her small family is safe, at least for now. But she is haunted by the memories of her father, his terrible death and how silently their mother slipped away, and mourns being expelled from Castile and the community she grew up in. It was always warm and comforting, even though Ledicia found her people too doctrinaire in their beliefs and practices. It was, however, a community she felt she belonged to. Now vanquished, she is reminded of the stark reality that being born a Jew is dangerous.

—

The merchant, Hazan is a man of middle age who has never married. As the years pass, his main interest and occupation revolves around the textiles he traffics throughout Europe which have made him a wealthy man. He is not interested in much of the household's business which he leaves to Gideon, who has been with the Hazan family since he was a young boy. Gideon takes care of both the inside and the outside of Mr. Hazan's large but modest family home, surrounded by sufficient acreage to keep flower and vegetable gardens, livestock, and a park containing lovely wooded footpaths.

Ledicia is treated well enough and finds Gideon to be a kindly steward. Her chores are light but never-ending. She must help in the kitchen, the laundry and see to it that the fires are lit in the occupied rooms. Making the beds and cleaning the chamber pots are her daily tasks. Shaking out the rugs on the floor of all fourteen rooms is done once every week. The rest of the household cleaning and cooking is left to others. One task she is occasionally given, is polishing the silver and brass, which is, by far, her favorite. It allows her to spend quiet time alone with her thoughts..

Her only complaint is that there is neither time nor books to read. At night, tired from her chores, she lies in bed composing poems as she watches the candle's flame lower and sputter out. In the darkness, she commits them to memory as she has no access to parchment, ink or quill.

"One day I will write them down. One day maybe I will have a home of my own."

Ledicia's days are long but not unpleasant. She is lonely, though she has on occasion been able to visit her brothers, or they have been free to come to her. They are growing taller and have become quite robust with the daily chores of the farm and are of an age that allows them to be more adaptable to change than Ledicia. They seem to be able to put aside the life they left behind. On the days of their visits, her smile returns and she is happy.

When she has been in service for a year, Ledicia is asked to run an errand that gives her the opportunity to venture outside the confines of the estate. She must deliver a parcel to the temple. It is a fine bolt of fabric for the new Rabbi's vestment. Happy for the chance to leave her household chores, she walks the few miles to the synagogue, delighting in the sense of freedom, and the warm, pleasant sun that heralds the coming spring. The parcel grows heavy, so she slings it over her shoulder and walks briskly down the road, stopping once in a while to rest and enjoy the flowers that line the path. Some are in full bloom, their fragrance intoxicating, others are still pushing their way up from the earth. She drops the bundle when she reaches the front gate of the temple, just in time to see a young man walking towards her. She quickly picks up the bundle and begins to turn away. He stops her and asks if he can be of help.

"Yes, please. Can you direct me to Rabbi Isaiah Avraham?" He politely says he can and asks if he might relieve her of her heavy bundle.

"Thank you, but I have very specific instructions. This must be given directly to the Rabbi."

He smiles before he speaks again. "Well then, as I am he, I can take it from you."

Ledicia blushes and gives him the bundle. For a brief moment their eyes lock in recognition. When she turns away, the Rabbi says,

"Stay a moment. I don't believe I have seen you at temple, may I ask your name?"

"Ledicia, Rabbi, sir, my name is Ledicia Serrano."

"Serrano! Are you any relation to Naftali Serrano?"

"Yes, he was my father."

8

LEDICIA AND ISAIAH

*I*T'S AFTERNOON AND *Isaiah has already had lunch and is sitting at his desk, waiting for the afternoon callers. Getting up he looks in the mirror examining his face. "I'm alright" he thinks, and begins to pace around the room, stopping at the window to enjoy the fulsome signs of spring. He wonders why it's so hard to concentrate. The spring air makes him lightheaded and nostalgic. As though something he wants is within reach, but doesn't exactly know what or where it is.*

In just a few minutes he will open his doors to members of his congregation who seek his council. Often the outer chamber is crowded, so the entire afternoon is spent advising people about marriage, dealing with a difficult neighbor, boundary disputes, or where to get a loan to buy a goat. He hears about a sick baby, or a marriage that is unhappy. His days are always full. It is only in the early morning hours, after a light breakfast, that he can take solitary walks which allow him to think and clear his head before he makes his house visits. The afternoons are full. Evenings, after dinner, are spent writing and reading and sometimes playing the piano.

There's little time to think about what is missing from his life, but lately he is taking his early morning walks to the merchant Hazan's house. While there, he inquires about Mr. Hazan's health and brings news of the progress on the synagogue's library building, to which Mr. Hazan has been a financial contributor. Isaiah is genuinely excited about this. The library will house the works of rabbinical scholars and archive the congregation's family information. But the real reason Isaiah is here, is the hope he will get a glimpse of Ledicia.

Setting out on this clear, cool morning in August, he is determined to find a reason to speak to Ledicia. Efron greets him warmly, inviting him to sit and share breakfast together. Isaiah accepts the offer, sipping a cup of coffee in Efron's Conservatory and begins his inquiry.

"How is your health? You look well."

"Indeed, I am" Efron laughs. patting his stomach.

"I've been meaning to ask you about the young woman from Castile, who is working in your employ."

Mr. Hazen stops to think. "Ah yes, you are speaking of Ledicia."

"Yes, Ledicia Serrano. Is it possible to speak with her?"

"Of course." He summons her immediately and when she appears, still drying her hands on her apron, Isaiah bows and asks Efron if she can be excused from her chores for a little while, explaining he has questions she might be able to answer. Mr. Hazan, good-naturedly shrugs his shoulders. "Of course, there is nothing urgent that must be done here."

Guiding Ledicia towards one of the paths in Hazan's park, they walk in silence at first. Ledicia is puzzled but does not speak. Finally, he turns to her and explains the reason for his visit.

"I know that your father was the well-known scholar, Naftali Serrano. I know his work and hear that his books were banned and probably burned in Spain. Do you know if there might still be copies? The reason I ask is that I would like to include them in our new library."

Ledicia hesitates to speak at first.

"I'm afraid all his books have been burned—thrown into the same fire that my father succumbed to when he was lashed to the stake."

Ledicia abruptly turns away. Isaiah winces but says nothing. Seeing the sudden slump of her shoulders, he understands the pain he has inadvertently inflicted upon her. Ledicia does not want to lie but does not want to reveal that she possesses the last book her father wrote. It is the only material link to her father. How can she give it away? She remains silent, but finally turns to Isaiah practically whispering.

"Before I left Spain, I hid his last book in my satchel. I was his helper, his scribe."

"*What! You, can write? Isaiah exclaims in amazement.*"

"*My father was my teacher.*"

"*But this is excellent. Do you know how unusual you are? And very fortunate too, I should say.*" *Then he looks at her earnestly,* "*But you mustn't let people know of your ability.*"

"*I know. I know. I do keep this to myself, but sometimes it's hard to hide.*"

"*I can understand how important the book is to you, but if you might ever consider lending it to our library, I will promise you this. I will take good care of it. Should you want it back, I will honor your request. I feel sure your father would be grateful that his work will be read.*"

—

The courtship begins slowly. In their now more frequent morning walks, Isaiah learns how keenly Ledicia wants to be able to read books.

"*There are no books in Mr. Hazan's house.*"

"*What would you like to read?*"

"*Almost anything—everything.*"

One day, Ledicia confesses that she composes poetry.

"*I would be honored if you would let me read your poems.*"

"*I cannot let you read them as I have not written them down. I have no paper or ink.*"

Isaiah thinks a moment and then, smiling says, "*Perhaps I can remedy that.*"

They spend the next few months meeting in this way, till one day, Isaiah has an idea and visits with Mr. Hazan again.

"*Mr. Hazan, would you allow Ledicia some time off, perhaps a few hours, one afternoon a week? I could use some help at the temple.*"

The merchant is not unaware of what has transpired over the last few months. With a twinkle in his eye, Mr. Hazan says,

"*Oh, I didn't realize you were shorthanded. How can Ledicia help you?*"

Embarrassed, Isaiah fumbles for an explanation. "*Well, there is the garden. The garden needs weeding and the vegetables…the vegetables need to be preserved for winter.*"

"*Ah yes, of course, the garden.*" *Efron lets Isaiah wait for his answer, feigning concern about giving up Ledicia's time for a few hours. He is just having some fun with the young Rabbi, before agreeing to give Ledicia the afternoon off.*

Isaiah approaches Ledicia with his real purpose, suggesting that she work in the library. The first task he gives her is to write out his sermons which are on various scraps of paper, notes jotted down as ideas come to him. He would like to expand, categorize and include them in a bound book.

Copying Isaiah's sermons, Ledicia becomes infatuated with Isaiah's mind and begins to feel a certain closeness to him. While working at the desk in the library, she's often distracted by the hope that Isaiah will visit her. On the frequent occasion when he does, he often looks over her shoulder to examine the progress of her work. She finds her heart beating just a bit more quickly when he is close. Sometimes he asks for her opinion. They seem to be of similar minds some of the time, and it is a relief to Ledicia that he is not disturbed that she can read and write and is capable of thinking abstractly, even when they disagree. She is amazed that he allows her to be his intellectual foil when they find themselves in serious discussions.

Ledicia begins to wait impatiently for Thursday afternoons. Not only is she able to practice her writing, but there are books in the library that she can read when she gets the chance and there is always the hope of seeing Isaiah. She becomes more careful about the way she looks, making sure she wears a clean apron and removes her cotton scarf allowing her hair to flow down her back, freshly washed and neatly tied. Isaiah too, looks forward to these afternoons, particularly when he can steal a few moments from his work to visit the library with the pretext of checking on the progress of her work. He knows one of the ways to her heart and one day surprises her with a sheaf of paper and ink, hoping the day will come when she will allow him to read her poems.

There is little doubt about Isaiah Avraham's intentions, and it is not a surprise that Ledicia is beginning to fall in love with him as well. There is a familiarity, a common thread that seems to tie them together. Not only did he arrive in Edirne from Castile at about the same time, but they both speak the curious language of their ancestors, and both have experienced the same discrimination and loss. His muscular youth, vitality, open-mindedness and generosity move Ledicia. Tall and energetic, with piercing dark eyes, she is often mesmerized when he looks directly at her. He is amusing and likes to have an argument even if he is in danger of losing it. He adores seeing Ledicia blush when he flatters her and enjoys her serious nature, delighted when he breaks through her serious disposition and makes her laugh. She has a lovely laugh. To his eyes, she is not only beautiful, but impressively graceful. He admires her active mind and wants to nurture it. Their bond feels strong, and on her 20th birthday Isaiah asks her to become his bride. On the day of their wedding, she presents him with a small book of poems. He accepts the book with exaggerated solemnity, trying to hide the smile that escapes from his happy face.

Madame Avraham stops her narrative, gets up and disappears into another part of the apartment. When she returns, she is wearing a pair of white cotton gloves and holds a small book in her hand. Laying it carefully on the table, she looks directly at Beka.

"This is the book of poems Ledicia gave Isaiah!"

Beka stares at the book and then at Madame. "I can't believe you have this." She walks over to the table to look at the small book with its worn leather covering. It looks like it will disintegrate if she breathes too heavily on it.

Madame opens the book to reveal lines of delicate handwriting. The small slanted letters are just visible, but Beka cannot make out the words.

"This is so beautiful" Beka cries. "What does it say? Is it written in Ladino? Can you read it? Madame?"

"Yes, it is Ladino – and yes, I can read it."

"Please, Madame, read one of the poems—or two?"

Rachael picks one poem and reads it first in Ladino and then translates it into English. The words flow easily. The syntax is complicated but original and beautiful. Ledicia's lyricism and voice are present, here in this 20th century room.

Binyamin Raphael Avraham

General Kristov

Battle of Tutrakan

9

EMERGING HEROES

DURING THE RUSSIAN-TURKISH war of 1877, Ruschuk, Bulgaria, now called Ruse, was nicknamed "Little Vienna," the showcase for the Ottoman Empire. That would explain, Beka reasons, why so many of the venerable buildings around the city look European, without the characteristic style of the Ottoman Empire or the brutal architecture of the Soviets. The city's proximity to the Danube transformed it into an international trading city with an important financial center. Even so, much of the population lived in poverty.

A day after their meeting with Rachael, still feeling the glow of Ledicia and Isaiah's beautiful love story, they get back to work. Sitting on a creaky bench at the Central Historical Archives, Beka and Michael are given gloves to protect the documents that are being brought to them. The librarian has placed a packet of documents on a special pad used for reviewing old books and documents. Two stories emerge from their reading that may be relevant.

Beka opens an 18th century document describing an occurrence towards the end of that century when the Jews from Edirne, Turkey, began to migrate to Ruse hoping to seek a better future. But by the 19th century the city is afflicted with plagues, fires and thieves. The region, in general, is in a constant state of flux, not uncommon in Bulgaria's history.

Beka turns a page in the chronicle that's been translated into English. In it she comes across the name of a Rafael Binyamin Avraham living in Ruschuk (Ruse) between 1800 and 1810. She stops reading when she sees the name. Can this be her great-great grandfather? His second child, Binyamin Rafael Avraham, born in 1823 might be her great grand-father and the subject of this chronicle. She reads that he apparently lived for eighty-seven years. "Oh, my goodness!" she cries out and turns to Michael. The other patrons look up, annoyed to hear their silence disturbed. Realizing where she is, she leans over to Michael, whispering,

"I think I found my great-grandfather. This document relates the story of how this guy helped save this city from being destroyed by the Turks during the war of 1877!"

The six-page account has been transcribed into English by relatives of the two men in the story and signed by them in 1948. It describes how the lives of the inhabitants of Ruschuk (as it was called by the Turks) were saved from slaughter on the 30th day of August 1877.

The war between the Ottoman Empire, (the rulers of the Balkan region at the time) and the Russians, break out in April of 1877 and most of the inhabitants flee the city. Many neighborhoods have already been destroyed. The war between the Turks and the Russians continues for months, but on the 8th day of February, 1878 the Turks officially surrender to the Russians. Beka remembers the sign in the park in Sofia, named Doctor's Park commemorated these battles and the medics who lost their lives.

The story in this document concerns two men, Ivan Vedar and Binyamin Rafael Avraham.

Ruschuk, Bulgaria
August 18, 1877

From the window of his shop, Binyamin looks out at the deserted street. There is a ghostly quiet hanging over the neighborhood. His shop still has shelves filled with jars of herbs, botanicals and potions, tallow candles and incense. Binyamin is well-known for his healing powers. He is a trusted and import-ant member of the community. Not so long ago, there were long lines of town folk with all sorts of ailments waiting to see him. He cured both peasants and royalty, but now there are few to cure. Most have left the city or died in the bombardments. Grimacing, he knows this is the way of life. One war after another. One country conquering another, as if another country's land is more precious than their own. It is an old story in this part of the world and he is weary of the struggle. He has stubbornly refused to abandon his home because this is the only life he knows, but even he is not sure how long he will be able to hold out. His wife is anxious to leave. They have argued about this every day for weeks. So far, he has remained intransigent, even while she cries, and pleads.

"Think" she argues, "of our children, I have seen enough of the barbarism of these men. We must find a place where it is safe for us all."

He loves his wife and all his children but feels this is their home and has been for a very long time. He wants to stay strong.

Still mulling over what to do, he sees a Turkish soldier heading towards the shop in a ragged uniform. Bowing slightly, Binyamin opens the door warily, and greets the soldier as he enters. Without a word the soldier takes off his shirt. He demands that Binyamin examine the mean-looking rash that has spread throughout his back. Recognizing this type of eczema, Binyamin makes up a cream of aloe vera, and prickly chaff flower, instructing the soldier to have it applied directly to his skin twice a day and if possible, bathe with vinegar regularly. Grateful, the soldier takes the cream, puts on his shirt and as he prepares to leave the shop, stops, and hesitantly looks, not at Binyamin, but at the floor. Under his breath he confides that his battalion and the remaining Turkish army have instructions to abandon the city to the Russians.

"Our orders are to kill any Bulgarian remaining in the city and burn their homes. We will be forced to retreat because the government does not want to leave anything behind for the Russians. The soldier continues, "Most of the younger Bulgarian men have already been taken into forced labor by the Russians for the purpose of strengthening the fortification around the city. There is no question that the Russians will be victorious."

With that, the soldier puts on his cap, lays a few coins on the counter, and leaves.

When he is out of sight, Binyamin locks the door of his shop and quickly walks the few blocks to his friend, Ivan Vedar's home in a section of town that has not yet been destroyed. Vedar is a language scholar and the founder of Freemasonry in Bulgaria. The ruling men of the city have always sought his council. Binyamin and Vedar are among the most respected Bulgarians in Ruschuk. When Binyamin cured Vedar of a persistent cough that had plagued him for months, he became a trusted friend.

After talking over the dire situation that the city is in, they call on a few other men and together hatch a plan to bribe the Turkish Military Governor.

Vedar, using his position as a Freemason, secures enough money in hopes of bribing the Turkish governor into canceling the planned destruction of Ruschuk. They are sure the Governor will be easily bribed and it is Binyamin's silky way with words that adroitly closes the deal. They convince the Governor that he will not only be extremely well off, but also remembered as a hero, and will, no doubt, have a statue erected in the main square to honor him. They successfully appeal to his greed and vanity. The Governor convinces the Turkish government to surrender peacefully to the Russians which thankfully leaves Ruschuk intact.

—

When Beka turns to the last page, her eyes widen in disbelief. There is a photograph of a man and a woman with a caption underneath. When she catches her breath, she nudges Michael.

"Check out this photograph, Michael. It's him. Binyamin Rafael Avraham and his wife. He looks like my father and his wife looks a lot like my aunts and a bit like my sister!"

The colorized photograph shows a man wearing a long coat trimmed in fur, under which he is wearing a long-skirted garment. He has a full white beard and is wearing a Greek captain's hat, which seems incongruous. The stout woman sitting by his side has a Mona-Lisa-like smile and wears an outfit similar to her husband's. On her head she wears a striped turban. Her jacket is fur-lined and beneath that, a long pale grey-green dress. The colors of their costumes are subdued, but they look like a lively pair.

This is the first document they have found with records of the Avraham family in Ruschuk during the 1800s. Beka and Michael, excited by this find, continue to search through records hoping to find more information about the role her family played in the history of this country.

They read a number of other documents, but find nothing. Disappointed they are about to end their search when Michael finds a document that strikes him as important. This one concerns a general. He recognizes the last name. Could this be Petya's grandfather? They have already learned that Beka's Aunt Irina, the sister of her father, and mother of Petya, married Gregor Kristov. Therefore, Gregor may be the son of General Kristov, named in this document. Though he is not a blood relative, Beka is fascinated by the possible connection. This document describes the events of the Second Balkan War of 1912 between Serbia, Greece, Romania and Bulgaria as well as the First World War.

Since the document is written in Bulgarian, Michael must translate it for Beka. Reading on, they learn that in the 1800s, the Romanians acquired military weaponry from Belgium and were able to annex a considerable portion of the northeastern part of Bulgaria along the Danube. Small countries like Bulgaria were often in danger of losing territory to one of the great powers. That is how the city of Tutrakan on the Danube in the region of Dobruja became the Romanians' military stronghold. This was devastating for the Bulgarians because the entire region supplied almost all the wheat for the rest of country. When Bulgaria finally entered the First World War, they took sides with Germany and Austria-Hungary, while Romania was an ally of the Western powers.

The Bulgarian government was determined to take back Dobruja and the city of Tutrakan from the Romanians. It was General Kristov, one of the top-ranking commanders, who successfully recaptured the region in 1916 during the height of that war.

As Beka listens to Michael, she feels sure they have hit upon another family nugget.

"General Kristov I believe is a relation, I think he is Petya's grandfather, the cousin we met last week!

"If these two men are even tangentially related to me, then I've just learned that I have a more interesting family than I ever imagined."

She circles back through her own life. How different the scale and texture has been compared to what she is learning about those who lived in this part of the world in former centuries. The historical facts are interesting, but what is missing, what Beka realizes she can never really know, is who these people were. Their deeds are recorded and speak for themselves, but what were they like as fathers, mothers, husbands, wives, and friends? Did they collect stamps, or enjoy propagating roses? Were they mean-tempered, kind or did they have a sense of humor. The true picture of their lives and loves, their joys, challenges and sorrows are not written, so she can only imagine what she will never know. Yet these stories and the photographs she is looking at, give Beka a narrative that her imagination can build upon.

Svishtov, Bulgaria
June, 1877

Pantelay Kristov runs home from school with a serious request he wants to discuss with his father. The town he lives in is a quiet, peaceful place, not suffering as much as the rest of the country. His home is in an upper-middle-class neighborhood far away from the neighboring cities' vicissitudes. He is determined to convince his father to send him to the new military school in Sofia, the one he heard about in school this morning.

The Russian-Turkish war that began in April is in full operation. Russia's goal is to free the Balkan nation from the yoke of the Ottoman Empire once and for all, and recently liberated the city of Svishtov. It is situated in northeast Bulgaria, on the banks of the Danube.

The impressionable Pantelay is sixteen, and often interacts with the Russian soldiers who have been using the town as their base. They are a rowdy bunch, friendly with the young teenager who likes to spend time around them. His enthusiasm and hero-worship amuse them, and they often spar with him. He loves the culture and camaraderie he observes among the soldiers. What he wants most is to become a soldier like them. Not just a soldier, but a commander. But he knows his father is determined that he honor him by becoming a scholar or a doctor. While he is an excellent student, eager to please his father and quick to learn foreign languages, his real desire is to become a great soldier, and takes every opportunity to pester his father and plead his case. Seeing the determination and single-mindedness of his son, his father reluctantly agrees to send him to the military school. Pantelay is surprised and overjoyed by his father's turnabout.

Dreaming daily of living and studying in Sofia, he begins to spend hours in the library reading about military conflicts throughout history and especially those in his own region.

This morning he wakes up, ready to send his application to the school, when he hears his mother crying. Startled, he dresses quickly and runs to his parents' room where his mother is sitting by his father's bedside. The doctor has just left and a priest has been called. Through tears and whispers, his mother tells her children who have all gathered in the room, that their father has had a stroke and is not expected to live. As they try to comfort her, they hold back their own thoughts and fears.

Although his father was known to be an astute businessman, he'd entered into a curious deal believing it would be profitable and would help support his son's desire to go away to school. He felt certain that he was making the right decision when he purchased a number of lavender farms, planning to manufacture and export lavender oil. The soil and climate, normally perfect for such a product, began to change due to an unusual weather pattern that hovered over the country for months. Then the war's blockade, prevented Bulgarian products from leaving the ports. His gamble was proving to be a disaster and he was in danger of losing most of his comfortable fortune. For weeks his father had been worried and depressed. His health slowly began to decline. He started eating food far too rich for his digestion and drank earlier and earlier in the day. Not able to overcome the strain of his defunct business, he lies in a coma, very close to death.

Despair grips the family and they take turns at his bedside, but within a few days after his father's stroke, Pantelay and his brothers become father-less sons and their mother becomes a widow, with an uncertain future. The unexpected timing of his father's death, and the family's financial difficulties end his dream of entering the Sophia Military Academy.

As the youngest brother in a family of five, Pantelay doesn't shoulder as much of the family burden as his two older brothers, but they all do their share of work to get through this time. His mother, still grieving, but with tenacity and clever management, along with a mind uncommonly gifted for business, keeps the family together. Pantelay looks at his mother with new appreciation as she takes over her husband's business, moves her family into a smaller house in a less desirable part of town. They go without expensive cuts of meat, mend their clothes rather than buy new ones. The cook and the maid are let go and the family, without complaint, become thriftier in every way. In the next year, life begins to return to normal and the family becomes accustomed to their new circumstance.

During the initial stressful year, the boys, still young, are able to remain playful. However, one fateful morning, Pantelay's older brother finds a revolver and while he tries to figure out how it works, accidentally shoots

Pantelay in the leg. The wound is both serious and painful and he is confined to his bed for months, enduring painful procedures and exercises. The medicines he takes are distasteful and he is put in daily warm bathes and slathered with ointments. His convalescence stretches out over months before the danger of infection finally passes and he can walk again.

This mishap, as well as his father's untimely death, might have had a defeatist effect on Pantelay, but the opposite is true. With his already pronounced streak of stubbornness, he develops a maturity that guides him through the year, determined to get well and achieve his goal of one day becoming a military officer. With his mother's excellent handling of her husband's business, she resuscitates their financial footing as well as gaining the absolute respect of her children. Three years later, in 1880 she sends Pantelay to the military school in Sofia.

He always knew he was destined to be a soldier and would rise high in the ranks. And he does. During the First World War, he is made a general. As he grows older, he becomes a relatively portly man, certainly not the figure of a dashing hero. Nevertheless, he is a brilliant strategist, a trait that will become instrumental in his career.

Tutrakan, Bulgaria
September, 1916

It was during the Second Balkan War, that the Romanians built a strong defensive line on the plateau around the town of Tutrakan to protect the river from enemy artillery. They built three rows of pitfalls and barbed wire connecting some of their forts where they stored their artillery. Guns and artillery were also kept on nearby islands in the Danube to support and protect Romanian ships.

During World War One, Bulgaria, determined to get their land back, train the Third Army for over a year and gather as much military equipment as possible. The intention is to protect the Danube's frontier. As the battle progresses, General Kristov, now the commander of the 4th Preslav Division, is put in charge of all the Bulgarian forces in the region.

Consulting the joint chiefs, who are all in agreement, The General issues an order to attack the Romanian defense of Tutrakan. Just before the order is to be carried out, Pantelay takes a second look at the game plan and unilaterally stops the order from proceeding. The joint chiefs are furious with him for defying them. But Pantelay has an uncanny sense of how the chessboard of war should be played. After a series of heated discussions and arguments that ensue, the joint chiefs reluctantly give in to the General's judgment. For days, Pantelay waits and watches the activities of the enemy and finally on the morning of September 6, 1916, decides the conditions are right and gives the order to begin the barrage.

In the face of the heavy Bulgarian artillery, the surprise attack leaves the Romanian soldiers without the ability to break-away or escape, allowing the Bulgarians to enter Tutrakan. and the Romanian soldiers surrender in large numbers. The speed with which the victory is achieved is unexpected, and while the Bulgarians fight bravely, they do lose a number of their own men in the battle. Nonetheless the victory boosts the morale of the Bulgarian soldiers and their allies. When the General reads the letter from the Romanian commanders, offering the unconditional surrender of all their men, and materiel, one hears a deafening cheer coming from his very tired battalion.

Years later, this battle will be examined in major military academies all over the world and the general becomes a well-known and respected commander. He is considered a hero in the city of Tutrakan and will be honored with yearly commemorations of the victory there. Streets and villages are named after him as far away as Varna, Ruschuk, and his hometown of Svishtov. While all of this attention and recognition is welcome, the General has only one regret, and that is that his father did not live to witness his achievement.

Michael continues to read the account of the General to Beka.

"He served in the military for thirty-three years. Before retiring he was given the highest honor the military can bestow: *General of the Infantry*. He lives another nine years after retiring to Sofia with his family and dies in 1927 at the age of 64."

Figuring out the date of his death, Beka calculates that Petya, his grandson, born in 1931, never had the opportunity to know his grandfather.

Now that pieces of her family's history are slowly coming together, Beka hopes they will, at some point, be able to put together a reasonable account. The project, though overwhelming, has already offered up some interesting surprises. More determined than ever, she hopes she can paint a significant portrait of both sides of her family. It seems to have begun with Ledicia Serrano and her brother's journey in the 15th century and will continue through to the Second World War to the present. Her mother's family also came from Spain, so the lives of the two families still need to be stitched together.

10

THE DINNER

FEELING CELEBRATORY AFTER their discoveries, they decide to treat themselves to a fine dinner at a restaurant recommended by the hotel's concierge.

Beka looks critically at her meager wardrobe. She only packed her ubiquitous jeans, one pair of dress slacks and a few sweaters for this trip. Because shoes take up so much space, she limited herself to a pair of boots and a pair of sneakers. She spends the next two hours in a shopping mall, trying on one dress after another, desperately hoping to find one she likes. She hasn't owned a dress in years. A dress means she must find a pair of shoes. Weary, after countless try-ons, she settles on a simple black dress and a pair of shoes with a higher heel than she normally wears. About to leave the store and enter the mall's large rotunda, she remembers she needs a pair of nylon stockings. Hurriedly picking up a pair, she almost reaches the exit when she passes a jewelry counter and impulsively chooses a pair of hoop earrings. The big question on her mind is whether she will get through the night without having to take off her new shoes. She'll bring her sneakers just in case.

The restaurant turns out to have just the right atmosphere and the menu is international. Over dinner, their conversation starts by considering what they have learned and how much more time they should spend in Ruse. Now that they have learned about Petya's grandfather, Beka is anxious to know if he can provide more personal details about his grandfather which means heading back to Sofia, but then they know there's more of Ledicia's story that might unfold. At least 300 hundred years to fill in. Michael understands that, but wants to return to Sofia soon because he has his own research to conduct at the Bulgarian National Library.

"You know, Michael, I haven't even begun to think about my mother's side of the family. I know less about them. I do know that my grandfather Samuel had blue eyes like my mother. Did his family leave Spain and go to Amsterdam first, and is it possible his family got mixed in with the Dutch? That seems highly unlikely…but who knows? And how did he get to Bulgaria? When and why?"

Michael, in his professor-of-history role, does his best to come up with a theory.

"The Portuguese began the expulsion of Jews a few years after Spain, and many of these Jews migrated from Portugal toward Central Europe and Amsterdam where they became very successful merchants. Perhaps your grandfather or his family traded in Eastern Europe, which may be the reason he or his family eventually settled here."

After dinner, Beka is feeling lightheaded from the three glasses of wine she drank. She realizes she's been wound-up tightly since arriving in this country. It is a mixture of the newness of the surroundings, her mission, and that she is here with a relative stranger. For the first time since they arrived, she is beginning to relax. When a strong double espresso is brought to the table after the meal, it occurs to Beka that she still knows very little about Michael. Something about him seems to have inhibited her from asking personal questions. But then she's always been shy about being too forward. She decided some time ago that people reveal themselves with time if you give them a chance. She figured he would do the same. But while he has offered bits of information, she has no idea what his life is about, and why he was willing to join her in this adventure. Feeling somewhat embarrassed, she is aware of how self-centered and pre-occupied she's been. She hasn't even asked him about his own research. Her own quest has superseded good manners and she failed to inquire about him or his needs. He's been more than a gentleman—patient, undemanding and helpful. Since he hasn't really been forthcoming about himself, she's made certain assumptions.

Twisting a slice of lemon rind into her coffee, Beka looks up at Michael, the wine loosening her inhibitions.

"So, Michael, I want to apologize to you for being so self-concerned. I think it's time I ask you more about yourself? Is that okay?"

"Of course, I'm an open book!"

"Really? Okay then, why are you here with me? I've never been entirely sure."

Michael smiles, leans over to get closer to Beka saying,

"Well…I wondered when you'd ask. The truth is, it occurred to me that there may be a book here. And I am due to write one."

"What kind of book?"

"I want to explore Bulgaria during the Ottoman Empire. Bulgaria during World War II, and Bulgaria after the war. There's been little written about it and maybe I might be able to incorporate something about you and your family."

"Me? My family!" Beka laughs, hardly able to hide how flustered she is. "It's too soon to know if there is anything about me or my family that is important enough."

"It's too early to know, that's true…but what we have come up with so far is interesting." Looking into her eyes, he reaches over and places his hand on Beka's. Startled, she instinctively withdraws hers and pick up her coffee cup. Michael still smiling, understands that Beka is uncomfortable. He finishes his coffee, picks up the check, signs it and gently guides Beka, now slightly unsteady, towards the bar.

"Let's end the evening with a digestive. Port or Brandy? He puts his arm around the back of her chair.

"Cognac please." She feels his closeness and isn't sure whether that makes her uncomfortable, but she is enjoying the attention, deciding she won't read too much in it.

"So, you want to know who I am and why I am interested in this project? It's very simple. I needed an excuse to come to Bulgaria. You showed up. Your family story interests me, and, well…don't be alarmed! Now I'm growing quite fond of you."

Beka feels the heat rise on her face. She stares into the glass of cognac as if she's trying to find a hidden message in the richly-colored liquid. She measures her response, avoiding the last part of what he said.

"You mean my family or specifically a more intimate history of the Spanish Inquisition?"

Michael picks up the conversation.

"Probably both, but not only that. I am Bulgarian, but not a Jew. What fascinates me is finding out more about the journey and the lives of the Jews that found themselves in the Ottoman Empire, and specifically in Bulgaria. I've never thought very deeply about it."

Hesitating for a moment, he takes a long sip of his drink and begins.

"Okay, here's what you probably want to know." He looks over at her and takes her hand. "Yes, I am married. I've been separated for several years. My wife lives in London, and is a mayoral director. We met at Oxford while we were both doing our graduate work. She was a political science creature and I was a history buff. We had a lot in common in those days, but as time went by, we grew apart. A distance we couldn't bridge. The good thing is that we are still friends, but no longer man and wife. However, we do have two grown children. A daughter and a son and a few grandchildren, all of whom still live in England. Her career and the children kept us from getting a divorce."

Beka perks up, now listening attentively.

"I've been a professor all my adult life…and I love teaching. I admit, after my wife and I separated, I felt unglued and couldn't figure out how to reinvent my life. When I was invited to come to America to join the faculty at the university, it felt like the right thing to do for both of us."

He stops talking, waiting for Beka to say something. She mumbles, "Oh, I see," but then remains silent, though still eager to hear more. He continues without a prompt.

"When you introduced me to your project, I felt a keen desire to return to my birthplace and the country where I earned my baccalaureate. I admit I was relieved to get back to England after my university experience here. The country was still under the heavy curtain of the Soviets. The color and vibrancy I'd always associated with this country had become dull. It made me quite sad. When the Berlin wall came down and the Soviet Union dissolved, Bulgaria began to change. I wanted to see this for myself. Also, and this is no small thing, I am eager to learn something outside of my usual concerns."

Beka says, feebly, "Those seem like very good reasons."

"Yes, that's it. In the process of getting to know you, I find myself attracted by your history and your earnestness. I like your spirit, and, well, your quirkiness."

Beka still playing with her cognac, looks at Michael with questioning eyes.

"Beka, please don't be concerned about me, or become skeptical. Not yet, anyway." He chuckles. "I'm really not a bad person and I can assure you, I am your friend."

Beka wants Michael to know that she does trust him. Her curiosity is heightened by what he just told her. She has so many more questions. She wants to know what his wife is like? Why had they become estranged? What do his children do? How old are they? How many grandchildren does he have? Is he involved in a relationship now? What exactly did he mean when he said he is fond of me?

Her facial expression seems to telegraph her silent questions.

"I am not a great mystery as I am sure you will learn." With that he gets up. "Come on, it's time to get some rest. Tomorrow is another day of discovery."

Walking back to the hotel, Beka is surprised that her feet do not hurt! Relieved to hear what Michael has revealed, she also knows something has changed. He walks her to the elevator and this time he picks up her hand, kisses it, and wishes her a goodnight!

—

She was delighted when she first saw the number of her room. The number eleven is boldly stamped in gold paint on the door of her hotel room. Eleven has always been her lucky number. Looking for connections and signs, she is sure it is a good omen.

Closing the door, she stops and leans against it, trying to figure out what she is feeling. Throwing off her shoes, she examines her face in the mirror above the sink and removes her makeup. Studying her face, she notices all the lines that have mysteriously developed. Where did they come from? Since her husband's death, she hasn't been paying much attention to the way she looks. Her eyes are still large and expressive, but her once long eyelashes seem to be disappearing and her full mouth now seems smaller and turned down by the force of gravity.

"Well, my dear" she says to the mirror, "you can't be confused with Sophia Lauren anymore!" She laughs out loud and heads for the shower.

A whole new set of thoughts drift in. It is hard to understand what significance any of what she is learning has and if and how it may have played a part in her own life which already has a long history. What crosses her mind is the thought that she may be the last period at the end of this family's sentence. And then, overlaying that thought, she wonders what role Michael will play in her life.

The shock of cold water abruptly ends her thoughts. She's been in the shower longer than the supply of the hotel's hot water allows. Shivering she puts on the hotel's bathrobe and folds herself into a chair as memories, years old, push their way forward.

February 16, 1961
New York City

Panicked, Beka stares at the test. It's positive. She is pregnant. "I'm not ready to become a mother!" Neither she nor her boyfriend, Lee, are ready or slightly interested in becoming parents. They both feel they are much too young.

Arriving at the doctor's office, she barely takes note of the assistant or the room where the procedure will take place. It all feels strange and deadly quiet. What frightens her is that strangers are about to perform a procedure that is hateful, intimate and deeply profound. She closes her eyes to avoid looking directly at them as they mechanically give her instructions. Otherwise, the only sound she hears are instruments being moved around on a metal surface.

Lee is waiting outside the building and his own nervousness compels him to walk around the block dozens of times. During one of the turns, he notices a gift shop and blindly picks out a gift…a large ashtray made of small orange and white mosaic tiles glued onto a black wooden plate.

Leaving the building, Beka is visibly shaken. They walk towards the subway and travel home in silence. Lying on the couch, she experiences some pain, not knowing if it is real or her mind cramping up. She begins to cry. Lee sets the gift down on the trunk which they use as a coffee table, and lies down next her. In this fitful moment of recognition, both understand the irreversible act they have committed.

It was as ugly an ashtray as she had ever seen but she kept it for years, perhaps to remind her of that day. Most often she pushes the incident into the farthest recesses of her mind, sometimes even forgetting the significance of that orange-tiled plate which eventually found its place under a potted plant where after years, deteriorates. She wonders if what she did on that day long ago, defines much of the way she has chosen to live. How different her life would have turned out if she allowed that pregnancy to go to term. But the what-if questions seem futile now. There are, she is sure, no what-ifs in life, but destiny already marked.

One of the main effects of the abortion is Beka's understanding that she will never do it again. She tries to keeps the experience buried in the place where she stores all her secrets. Years later, this time married, she becomes pregnant again. There isn't any question this time that she will finally become a mother. While the marriage does not last, her role as a mother nourishes and fulfills her though it was and still is sometimes a lonely journey. After she left Lee, he became quite successful and went on to marry twice and had six children. She often thinks of their child, The one that might have been, the one they never allowed to become.

What she will never have, is an opportunity to bask in the role of a matriarch surrounded by a large family. This is another part of life that up till now never concerned her, except perhaps when she witnesses other people's joy—their sense of belonging that comes from being surrounded by lives they had a hand in creating. Too tired to give her thoughts anymore time, she climbs into bed and turns out the light.

Petya's painting

11

THE PAINTING

Sofia, Bulgaria
September, 1945

Returning to Sofia from their internment in September of 1945, Petya and Irina are allowed to move back into their villa. Gregor joins them. Their grandmother is still there. Maria remains in Italy where she will eventually become a citizen. Due to the occupation, the condition of the building is shabby, looking very different from the day they were forced to surrender it. The occupying military had not been particularly respectful to their gracious and comfortable home. Gregor joins his wife and son and together they do what they can to bring their home back to its former beauty. They clean up the overgrown garden, throw away broken furniture, beat out the rugs and clean and polish all the furniture's surfaces, try to remove the scratches and restore the wood as best they can. Removing the stains left on the upholstered furniture is a chore that's far more challenging.

*Even though the war officially ended in May, the political situation in
Bulgaria is tense. The Communists are now in power and brutally suppress
any opposition. Gregor, relieved to have survived his incarceration is able
to go back to work in the textile industry which hasn't yet become nationalized. Petya goes back to school. However, life as they knew it, is a distant
memory. There are long lines for everything because there is a shortage of
everything. Finding decent food is a daily struggle. Legal matters, as well as
other transactions are tied up in a dizzying tangle of red tape which often
require waiting hours, days and sometimes months, without any guarantee
of satisfaction. People are becoming disheartened, fearing that this is how life
will be from now on. The bombed-out parts of the city are in disarray. Still,
given what they have been through, the family is happy to be back together
in what had been their summer home.*

*The months of internment caused Petya's school work to suffer and he
must work hard to catch up, but he is a bright, spirited lad and holds onto
the feeling that everything will get better. His optimism isn't rewarded.*

*In the summer of 1947, more than a year after they have been living in
the villa, the government, without warning, confiscates it. The notice they
receive reads quite simply;*

**"You have 24 hours to evacuate the premises. You may not take
any furnishing or possessions."**

*The government permits the family to move into one of the rooms in
their apartment in Sofia, but the rest of the apartment is used by the Bulgarian Telegraph Agency and their villa becomes the residence of the Interior
Minister. They have a hard time accepting the fact that their villa and all
their belongings have been summarily taken away and that they have no
recourse. This is now the new Russia-Bulgaria.*

Sofia, Bulgaria
February, 2003

"But now here I am. Back in this house after so many years!" Petya
looks around the living room and makes a sweeping gesture. Our villa was
returned to the family, more or less in tact in the early 90s when Bulgaria
was no longer part of the Communist bloc of countries. But I can tell

you, during the Communist occupation we were all very dejected knowing how powerless we were, and that we knew worse was yet to come."

The cold rain which began earlier in the day has not let up, but settling in the cozy living room, they warm themselves in front of a blazing fire. In this, their second visit, Beka, Michael and Petya have begun to feel like old friends. Beka studies Petya's face. He doesn't resemble the paternal side of the family. His strong, pleasant face shows signs of age. He's lived long enough to tell his story in an almost matter-of-fact way, but it's clear that those years changed his perspective. At the same time, it seems to have made him strong, but he seems to have retained his gentle nature.

Sofia, Bulgaria
March, 1947

Their apartment building is in an excellent location, situated in the center of Sofia, right in front of the Parliament building. While they are forced to live in cramped quarters, they are thankful that they are able to get around the city easily. Three of them live in one room and they also have a large bathroom which they use as a make-shift kitchen as well. Petya's grandmother is given the pantry where there is room for a single bed. This is a bitter ending to the life she'd become accustomed to as the wife of a national hero. Her husband, the General, died twenty years ago and she's thankful he did not live to see what is happening to his beloved country.

By 1950, all industries are nationalized, forcing Gregor out of his job. Now he must find ways to scrape together a living by securing translating assignments for the government. Speaking four languages fluently is a great help. Having been a successful lawyer and businessman, this new identity is demoralizing and begins to affect his health.

Petya is not allowed to study at the university. Instead, he is forced to spend two months in a work brigade, along with two hundred youths, assigned to the task of digging ditches for a factory sewage system that synthesizes fertilizer. For over eight hours each day, the brigade of Bulgarian youths is forced to dig large trenches, given only picks and shovels. The hours are long and it is very hot and humid. After spending the whole day at it, Petya watches as gushing water flows back into the trenches they have just finished digging. The walls collapse because they have not been fortified. One by one all the trenches they spent days digging collapse. He curses the ersatz Russian engineers who refused to provide the resources needed to fortify the trenches, and now the brigade is forced to dig them out all over again.

Exhausted and depressed, Petya counts the days when his two-month assignment will come to an end and he can return to his family. On the very day he returns home, he receives a directive from the government that the family must vacate their rooms within three days, and leave the city. Devastated by the whims of this government, but no longer surprised by its callousness, they head for a small town in Northern Bulgaria where other families have also been interned. They rent three rooms in a farmhouse that has neither running water or an indoor toilet. The pig stye adjacent to the walls of their rooms create an overwhelming stench which they can do nothing to eliminate.

No sooner have they settled, in than Petya receives a letter commanding him to report for military service. It's been years since the big war was over, but it is clear that Bulgarians have not yet been freed from the bondage of this government.

Petya spends the next years in the army. As a Bulgarian he is seen as a second-class citizen. Right from the beginning he is insulted and his minor complaints ignored. To make matters worse, his vanity is offended when his head is shaved and he is given an ill-fitting, shabby hand-me-down uniform. The pair of used boots are much too small and when he complains, the Sergeant looks at him with a sneer on his face and responds by saying,

"No, the boots are not too small, your feet are too damn big."

After enduring a few years of army life, he is finally assigned to a one-year course in chemical weaponry and sent to the town of Karlova, where for the first time, he is treated respectfully by his fellow soldiers. Oddly enough, this is where Petya begins to paint for the first time. When he learns that artists are needed to paint the rooms and barracks with colorful banners and scenes depicting the glories of Russia, he offers his service, claiming that he can draw. He hopes, by doing this, he will be allowed to skip the annoying field exercises and when he is given the job, he is surprised at how well he can draw. In no time his reputation spreads among the soldiers and soon he is busy filling not only the soldiers' orders but private peoples' as well.

Sofia, Bulgaria
February, 2003

Quite suddenly, Petya gets up and leaves the room. Michael and Beka look at each other, not sure why. He calls to them from the other end of the house, asking them to follow him. They walk tentatively down a corridor and enter a room which is filled with at least thirty beautiful framed watercolors.

"You know, painting runs in our family. We have many fine artists who are recognized. Do you paint, Beka?"

"No, I can't say that I have any talent. I dabbled when I was a teen-ager, painting ballet dancers and horses. I wasn't very good and I was more interested in dancing. Are these yours? They are marvelous."

Petya removes a painting from the wall, and hands it to Beka.

"This one is for you…to remember me by. Take it with my blessings and affection. I painted this one years ago when I was invited by the town of Tutrakan to be present during a celebration honoring my grandfather."

Beka accepts the painting, staring at Petya with surprise and delight. She remembers what she recently read about Petya's grandfather and how he took back the town from the Romanians during the First World War. The gesture so surprises her that she is almost speechless. She manages to blurt out, "I will treasure this." She doesn't realize how broadly she is smiling until she look at Petya and then to Michael and sees they are smiling too.

Petya seems pleased with himself. "Since my army experience revealed my ability to paint, I have been painting ever since. Come let's return to the warm living room and I will finish my story."

Sofia, Bulgaria
Late 1960s

The Communist government in Sofia decide they must compete with the capitalist countries by creating the Ministry of Science and Technical Progress. They hope to gain intelligence about western technology. That ministry is temporarily using Petya's family's old apartment in Sofia, where the Bulgarian

Telegraph Agency had once been housed–the same apartment they were so gracelessly evicted from by the government.

The Ministry begins recruiting the best professionals in the industry, with one important requirement: the ability to speak English, German, French and Italian. Petya is hired by Comrade Balevski, who has no idea that his new-hire is the former owner of this confiscated apartment.

Spending the next four years in the service of the Ministry, Petya enjoys his new station in life. The work and the intrigue of being part of the coun-terintelligence arm of the agency suits his fancy. He has been given a few curious assignments to spy on the British, both in Bulgaria and in Moscow. He feels as though he is a character in a movie and does not take his work too seriously. Petya produces very little worthwhile information from any of these KGB assignments, thus they are not very pleased with him. But as long as it lasts, he figures he will enjoy the status he is given and play along with their intrigues.

One day while at work, he is summoned to a hospital at the other end of the city where his father has been taken. Not yet an old man, his father has been weakened by his imprisonment and the ensuing years of stress under Soviet rule. Petya rushes to the hospital, but by the time he gets there, it is too late. His father died only minutes before.

Losing his father is the culmination of all the events he has experienced over the years. He is convinced that he must leave Bulgaria. But getting out of the country is not an easy thing to accomplish. The Soviets allow very few people to leave the country, and the currency is not recognized outside of Bulgaria. His mother, knowing she will be left behind is sympathetic and becomes his co-conspirator.

His sister, Maria, never left Italy, finishing her schooling there and has no desire to return to Bulgaria. Petya decides, therefore, that Italy is the logical place to start a new life. Getting there will be the challenge.

12

GOODBYE BULGARIA

BEKA AND MICHAEL spend one more afternoon with Petya. Happy to see them, he greets them warmly, this time bringing out a pot of tea. Apologizing, he says that wine is no longer good for him.

"It's a damn nuisance. The consequence of age, I suppose. But I can bring out a bottle if you like."

Not wanting to make him feel worse than he might already feel, both Michael and Beka almost simultaneously say that tea is fine.

Beka hands Petya a box. "See, I've even brought a tin of biscuits."

Since it snowed the day before, they resume their spot in his lovely living room and Petya, after asking how their work is going, falls right back into his story.

Sofia, Bulgaria
March, 1964

After the funeral and his final goodbye to his father, Petya is determined to leave Bulgaria for good. Living under the governing rule of Russia is and always will be oppressive. His father suffered from their treatment and died much too young because of it.

Months pass before Petya's formal petition, requesting permission to take a trip to Italy is even acknowledged. He is, however, suspicious when he receives a notice that he is to report to the Minister of the Interior in person. That seems very unusual. When he arrives, he is greeted politely before being drilled with a series of questions, many of them, he is sure, are meant to trip him up.

"Why does your sister not visit Bulgaria? Isn't she married to a well-known journalist?" Why not have them come here so they can write about

the great things happening in Bulgaria? How old are you? Why, aren't you married?"

Petya plays along with this interrogation and promises to persuade his sister and her husband to come to Bulgaria, and then lying, says, in fact, he is engaged and planning to marry in the Fall. His answers are apparently good enough, and his exit petition is approved.

He packs his belongings and stuffs them into all the pockets, crevasses and the trunk of his car. Before leaving in the early morning hours, he and his mother discuss the various ways he will try and get her out of the country.

His first hurdle will be the border custom station in Kalotino, Yugoslavia. Passing that easily, the next stop is Belgrade and finally Trieste. He makes it through all three and begins to relax, tasting what freedom feels like.

Arriving in Rome, his sister does not greet him warmly. She is not shy about displaying her discomfort.

"This apartment is too small for you to stay for any length of time. Besides you're not even documented, so how will you get a job? The economic situation in Italy is terrible." She is now and has always been pragmatic and unemotional.

Her sharp comments temporarily make Petya lose much of his new-found joy, but he is determined not to return to Bulgaria.

Legalizing his stay in Italy will be almost impossible. Luckily, an acquaintance invites him to stay in his beautiful apartment where he has the luxury of considering his options. Meeting a friend who recently left Bulgaria, also running into the same problem of lack of money and a proper visa, decide it might be easier and faster to get recognition status in Germany as political refugees.

Petya is reluctant to leave the beautiful apartment in Rome, but puts that aside and turns his attention to his next destination, Salzburg.

*Getting through Austria will be a problem. His passport explicitly states he is only visiting Italy. Fortunately, his passport is written in ink. The way to solve that problem (he hopes) is to forge his passport by adding the words, "Italy **and Austria.**" Unsure if this will pass, he is nervous about getting caught. His luck holds and they are free to enter Austria and from there to Germany and the central refugee camp near Nuremberg.*

Petya has arranged to meet a German friend and her parents in Austria. They plan to stay at a hotel close to the German border, where Petya will leave his car. There is a forest path not far from the hotel which crosses a border that is not guarded. Setting off on foot, Petya and his Bulgarian friend reach the main road, relieved to see that the median line on the road is painted white. They'd been told that if the median line is white, they are in Germany, but if it is yellow, they are still in Austria. Meanwhile, the mother drives Petya's car into Germany at a planned meeting spot. Everything goes smoothly, and the next day Petya and his buddy drive into the refugee camp where they spend a month before becoming officially recognized as political refugees. The possibility of freedom once again washes over Petya. Now he is convinced that he will be the author of his destiny.

The next years take him on a twisted path from a job with an architect, designing large public interiors, to becoming a graduate student at the University of Munich's Institute for Wood Research and Technology. There he finishes his doctoral work, but realizes he is not cut out for an academic life. His degree leads to what will become his life-long work in the timber industry and he establishes permanent roots in Switzerland where he meets his future wife and eventually where his mother joins him.

Petya stops talking and sits back quietly sipping his tea. "Bulgaria is the country of my birth and a place I loved till the war completely rearranged my life, but I am grateful. I have no regrets at all. Once the Berlin Wall came down, the family home was returned to the family, and I am thankful for that too. But it is in Switzerland that I met my wife and raised my daughter. My mother enjoyed being a grandmother and never returned to her homeland. It is in Switzerland where I have been happy. Life, after all, turned out very well. I consider myself a lucky fellow. But when my wife died ten years ago, I decided to commute, living in this house for a few months, and in Switzerland the rest of the year. When I reflect upon the journey of my life, I feel damn lucky."

"Petya. You've had an amazing life, and I thank you for sharing it with me. When I listen to your story, I reflect on how resilient and capable people can be if they have a strong enough spirit to persevere. Do you suppose the war made you stronger?

"It made me aware that you cannot take anything for granted. I learned that life can change at any moment. Turns out there are only a few options. One is to let it defeat you and the other is to push forward and grab on to all the happiness you can find. Most important, you must try to make every day worth living."

"It is clear that you have done just that. I am so happy I had this chance to spend some time with you. By the way, when you mentioned your sister, Maria, it reminded me that I did meet her when I was in High School. She just arrived in New York and my parents took her under their wing. She was older than me so I didn't pay much attention to her, though she was a frequent visitor in our house. I thought she was a rather plain young woman who wore cardigans and shapeless skirts. Her hair was held back with bobby pins. I don't think she thought much of me either. Once she got married and returned to Rome, I was amazed to see how good-looking and chic she had become."

Laughing, Beka notices the gold band still on his left hand. Though his wife has been dead for years he still keeps it on his finger. He reaches out with that hand and fondly pats her on the cheek whispering, "I do believe you have taken after your mother."

Leaving Petya's house, a mixture of happiness and a deep penetrating sadness comes over Beka. Happy because she has finally spent real time with her cousin and is beginning to feel like a member of a real family. Sad that it has taken so long, wondering if this will be the last time that she will ever see him. He is growing old.

Heading towards the car, Beka is holding the painting in one hand resting against her body and with her other takes Michael's hand. A very different sort of hand. Softer and with longer fingers. He squeezes her hand, which resembles her mother's, and kisses her on top of her head. Opening the door of the car with a gallant gesture, he takes the painting from Beka and stows in the backseat. Michael believes he understands what Beka's face is expressing. He sees not only a warmth and tenderness for Petya, but in this moment a tenderness for all mankind.

Beka's parents wedding

13

MARGOT

IT WAS JUST a week ago, while spending time with Petya, Beka learned that her mother's cousin Margot Davoud is still alive and living in the Paris suburbs. (Her name was Mati David, but her parents changed it—to pass as non-Jews when they left Vienna and fled to France at the start of the war.)

After their meeting with Petya, she contacted Margot and made arrangements to visit. Knowing even less about her mother's family than her father's, Beka welcomes the opportunity to become acquainted with Margot.

Beka puts down the telephone.

"Do you know it takes thirty-six hours to get to Paris by train, and only three by plane?

"I won't be going with you on this jaunt." Michael says distractedly. I have things I need to take care of. If it was me, I'd probably fly."

Beka considers her choices. She is conflicted between wanting to see the countryside of Romania, Hungary, Vienna, parts of Germany, and France before reaching Paris in three days, or the prospect of being in Paris in just three hours. And what will Michael be doing, she wonders? But she brushes that inconvenient thought from her mind.

So, she thinks, *it looks like I'll be taking this trip alone.* Beka doesn't ask why he will not be going with her, nor does she feel compelled to spend every moment with him. In fact, this trip will give her time to figure out what, if anything, she is beginning to feel about him. Content to spend time alone in Paris, she decides to fly, excited to reacquaint herself with the city where she spent so much time with her husband. She knows the language well enough to get by and is familiar with the layout of the city. She also feels being alone is somewhat liberating.

She's often been extolled as a free-spirit, but she knows she doesn't always feel that free. There is a definite resistance in changing this working relationship. At the same time, she is not sure why. A mixture of not wanting to rearrange her life and, perhaps, a reverence for the memory of her husband.

—

Stepping out of the taxi, she smells the familiar air of Paris; baguettes baking, roasting chestnuts and lavender. Confronted by so many memories, tears burn her eyes as she fumbles in her purse for cash to pay the cab driver. Before entering the hotel, she stops and stands in front of the hotel's door. The couscous restaurant is still on the ground floor where, as she recalls, one still checks in, and she notices that the outdoor area, where breakfast is served has a new awning. Notre Dame is visible in the background. The building is ancient and narrow. Checking in, she carries her luggage up the five flights of irregular and winding stairs, remembering these stairs were not her favorite part of this hotel. Reaching the top floor, out-of-breath, her luggage in tow, she is rewarded when she enters the spacious, bright room with the lovely view of the neighborhood. This is not the first time she's been in this room. The same red curtains hang in front of the big windows and the painting over the bed hasn't changed. A heart-clutching sadness assaults her. Beka looks up at the old ceiling beams. It just as she remembers it. Dropping her bags, she sits on the bed to catch her breath.

Beka's room in Paris

7^(th) Arrondisement, Paris, France
August 5, 1995

Exhausted from the flight, they practically fall into bed the moment they enter the room. As usual, Beka can only sleep for about an hour, much too excited about being in Paris, while her husband can easily sleep all day. Getting up, she finds her camera, noticing that her sleeping husband and the room will make a fine photograph. Her husband's bare back, peeks out from the disheveled bedclothes, casually draped around him, the imposing lady in the painting above the bed, sits at an outdoor café reading the newspaper. The red curtains on the windows billow into the room. She will encounter this photograph every time she turns on her computer.

—

Paris, France
February, 2003

Changing into more comfortable clothes, Beka leaves the hotel very early the next morning and walks to her favorite bookstore, Shakespeare and Company, only a few blocks away. The narrow aisles filled with books from floor to ceiling are hardly wide enough for a person to walk through. A settee pushed up against a corner nook is often used by homeless poets who need a nap. Books are piled on the floor all around other settees and crammed into dozens of shelves. A side door leads to a set of stairs to the upper floors that have more rooms filled with books. The second-floor landing is narrow and opens onto a large room with a long table in the center and rows of folding chairs leaning against the wall. At the moment the room is empty. It is often the room where people meet or authors read from their newest book. It's a wonder the building hasn't collapsed from the weight of books, or burst into spontaneous flames. Beka, unable to focus on a particular book, picks up a 630-page biography of Mary Shelley. The inside title page has the Shakespeare and Co. stamp imprint which is enough reason to buy the book. Walking a short distance, she breathes in the life of the city, finds an empty table at a nearby café, and orders a coffee. This is the city she hoped she would live in one day. But that hope died with her husband's untimely death. After nursing her coffee as long as possible, she reluctantly leaves the café and takes the metro to Parc de Bagatelle. Peacocks take possession of the walkways, claiming them their private esplanade. A footbridge takes her to a small almost hidden man-made grotto filled with water that gurgles over the stones. The outline of the city's buildings is visible around the perimeter of the park's expansive green lawns. Beds of daffodils seem to wave a personal welcome. It's a lovely walk-through and Beka is bathed in sweet nostalgia.

Before the afternoon ends, she heads for l'Hotel des Invalides to revisit Bonaparte's tomb so she can walk around the cluster of museums in these massive baroque structures which once accommodated the wounded soldiers of the war of 1812. She recalls sitting in the large chapel, Napoleon's tomb displayed prominently, listening to a Swedish pianist. Today the chapel is quiet except for a few tourists. She ends her day with a steaming bowl of couscous, lamb and vegetables at her hotel's restaurant.

The next morning, Beka takes the rapid transit to Orsay and knocks on Margot's door. Margot at 72 years is a tall, elegant woman. Comfortably, yet, fashionably dressed.

"Ah, Beka, bonjour. Ca va? Come in. *Je crois que tu ressembles à ta meré!*"

"Yes, I've been told that? Do you remember her?"

"No, not very well, but I see the facial features of our family."

Offering Beka a strong cup of coffee, they sit in Margot's sunlit kitchen surrounded by walls of blue and white tile and hanging copper pots. Engaged in small talk, they begin the task of becoming acquainted. Beka's thoughts and impressions are swirling around in her as she tries to concentrate on their conversation. How curious, it seems to her, there are people still alive who were part of her mother's life. People she didn't know existed. Their lives had at least for a time, run parallel with her own, but hold memories of her mother's life. A part of life she had no part in. Beka always assumed, as she supposed was true of most children, that her parent's lives only began when she was born. Why had she never given much thought to all the critical moments of her mother's life? She always assumed she was not that self-centered…and yet, aware of the irony, she has finally come to realize how real all the lives she is learning about are, and how they are connected, even in a distant way, to her own.

Checking the time, Margot suggests they pick up some groceries for their evening meal before the shops close at midday. Beka is delighted at how French Margot's habits are! But this should not be surprising, as Margot has lived here for the major part of her life. Shopping daily is a practice that is integral to the French. Fresh food is always the most important ingredient.

The next few hours are taken up with shopping. Beka delights in the culinary adventure as they stop in one specialty shop and then another to find the very best of what Margot plans to cook. Taking a long walk along the Bievre River, Beka asks to stop at a church so she can light a candle. It is a practice she started years ago while visiting the ancient churches in her travels. She always says a small prayer or wish…this time her wish centers around Michael. By the time they return to Margot's apartment, Beka is tired and falls asleep on the terrace, still wearing her coat. She wakes up suddenly very cold as the sun has grown weaker, smelling the delightful aroma coming from Margot's kitchen.

"Margot, I bet you're an excellent cook! When she tastes the Tournedos that sit so invitingly on her plate, she nearly swoons. The beef is tender and the delicate flavor of wine and herbs and butter remind her of how much she loves French cooking.

"Margot, I am enjoying this meal more than you can imagine."

The dinner is creating the same joy Beka has felt before. A feeling of having come home. A happiness she always feels when she is in France where food is almost an artform. There is a familiarity she can never quite explain. Even Margot's surroundings add to the old-world grace that is a reminder of where Beka came from. A special kind of charm and civility bred in the bone.

It is only after dinner, settling around the glow of an open fire that Beka tries to steer the conversation towards Margot's life in a way that doesn't feel like an interrogation.

"I guess you knew my mother when you were both very young?"

"Your mother was ten years older than me. Truth is, I only have one clear memory of her. It was during a visit when I was nine years old. She arrived with her family as they did every year for their month-long sojourn to Vienna and had already secured a season box at the Opera House."

"Oh," Beka interrupts. "That makes sense! That's probably the origin of my mother's devotion to Opera."

"Probably so, but you see, I was much younger and she really didn't pay much attention to me, so we never talked to each other."

"Did that bother you?"

"Not really. I was a child. I expected to be ignored! I do remember being quite taken by her. I thought she was very pretty, slim and always wore such beautiful frocks. I wanted to be like her."

"Beautiful frocks! That's true. My mother always looked elegant. I have a framed photograph of my mother and father's wedding portrait that hangs on a wall at home. To my eyes, her wedding gown is still the most beautiful one I've ever seen. It was made of a heavy silk crepe that clung to mother's tall slim frame—the gown spilled down her body like a waterfall into a pool of silk around her feet. She did not wear jewelry, and there were no sparkly things sewn into the gown. The simplicity was breathtaking. Long flowing sleeves covered her arms and a high-collared thick silk braid encircled her neck. She wore a modest veil and all that adorned her gown was the spray of white flowers she carried in her hands that cascaded down like a river of white buds. She looked like the movie stars of her day. My father too, looked handsome in his long-tailed tuxedo. I never thought of my father as really handsome, yet in this photograph, he is." Beka takes a breath, realizing she interrupted Margot. "I'm so sorry, my mind drifted…please go on."

"No don't apologize. I like to hear these things. I'll try and start from the beginning. I was born in Vienna, the daughter of your mother's paternal uncle. My father managed the family's large real estate concern. It made us all quite wealthy and I was a pampered child, until things began to change. The Vienna I knew by 1940 had turned hostile. Jews could no longer own businesses or property. Not only were we no longer welcome in our country, but it was becoming dangerous."

Placard in front of Hotel Excelsior, Nice France

Vienna, Austria
March 12, 1938 - 1943

Victor puts down the newspaper and gazes with unseeing eyes at a painting of a village street in Bulgaria. The article he just read unnerves him He is afraid their lives are about to change in unimaginable ways. The German army has marched into Austria accompanied by Hitler himself. His intention is to unify Austria and Germany. The paper calls it the "Anschluss" (meaning the political union between Germany and Austria.) Victor wonders what this will mean for his family and for his businesses. He is aware that the Jews in the city are already being discriminated against. His own real estate concern will likely be taken from him. Brooding on the possibility that he will lose everything; he attempts to keep his concerns to himself as if nothing has changed.

Only days after the Anschluss, Chancellor Schussnigg is replaced. While Schussnig accepts that Austria is now a German state, he strongly opposes the possibility that Austria will become part of the Third Reich. He cannot submit to their philosophy of racial superiority. His defiance gets him removed from office. The new Chancellor, appointed by Hitler, is in lock-step with the Third Reich. There is little to suggest that things will improve.

Zitia, his wife is not ignorant of what is going on and yet both she and her husband try to remain calm and not reveal their anxiety to their daughter Mati. But Zitia is quick to lose her temper and often cries herself to sleep. Everything becomes increasingly difficult. Now they are forced to wear gold stars whenever they are out-of-doors. Jews can no longer keep their stores open. They are not allowed to buy provisions at most of the other shops. Mati, is being shunned by the classmates she thought were her friends. Victor can't ignore the fact that they are in danger, but still refuses to believe anything really terrible will happen. And then it does. On the night of November 9th through the 10th, synagogues are torched, Jewish homes vandalized, schools and business destroyed. In Germany one hundred Jews are killed. "Kristolnacht" (The Night of Broken Glass) is the beginning of the violence conducted by the Nazis, who have begun to implement what they call, "The Final Solution."

These events cannot be ignored. Jewish businesses are forcibly confiscated, people are being rounded up and shot or taken away. Fear grips the whole family and it is clear they must escape.

In the early summer of 1940, the David family, along with 100,000 Viennese Jews secretly leave the city for different parts of Europe. The Davids pack what they can; jewels, a few rugs, and clothing and some family heirlooms and important papers and take the treacherous journey to Nice, not knowing if they will ever be able to return.

Though most of France is occupied by the Germans, Nice is still an unoccupied zone and reputed to be a safe haven for Jews.

Zitia is so despondent that she isn't much help. The combination of fear and loss temporarily paralyzes her. When they arrive in Nice they are crowded into a small pension for days, a situation they find suffocating after living in the luxurious large apartment they had to abandon. Eventually Victor finds a small apartment on a back street, not far from the waterfront. In order to pass as non-Jews, they change their names from David, to Davoud. While Victor feels comfortable keeping his name, their daughter, Mati becomes Margot, and Zitia, is Zoe. Victor finds work, earning a few francs by keeping the books for a few local businesses. They are fortunate to also have the money they were able to take with them. Nonetheless, they must learn to live frugally, a condition no different from everyone else, as the war accelerates throughout Europe.

Nice remains relatively peaceful for the next year. There is a shortage of food and dry goods, but the air is clean, the sea breezes comforting and the climate agreeable. There is, however, an undercurrent of fear and paranoia that drifts over the city. Furtive conversations. Cautious friendships.

By 1942 all of France is occupied by Germany and Italy. Nice falls under the control of Mussolini, which is fortunate because he does not have an interest or inclination in exploiting and identifying Jews or depriving them of their possessions or their lives as the Vichy government has ordered.

The Davoud family feel moderately safe and live as quietly as possible. Things change radically when on September 8, 1943 Italy surrenders to the Allied forces and Mussolini is no longer in power. Germany takes over the occupation of Nice and sets up headquarters at the Hotel Excelsior. It doesn't take long for SS officers to start rounding up any one suspected of being a Jew, eventually sending over 2000 to death camps.

Their landlady is a Vichy sympathizer and is suspicious of the Davoud family, so reports them to the authorities, believing she will gain some favor from the Germans if she cooperates with them.

In the early morning hours, three officers bang on the Davoud's door and without a warrant, arrest them and bring them to the Hotel Excelsior. Left in an empty room they are forced to stand for hours before finally being ushered into the ground floor office of the commandant where they are grilled with a prescribed list of questions. Victor does most of the talking. He has rehearsed this scene many times.

"How long have you lived in Nice? Where were you born? What is your occupation? What church do you attend?"

After answering all the questions, the commandant suddenly gets up and leaves the room. They sit perfectly still, looking at each other, obediently waiting for something to happen. After an hour, Zitia/Zoe gets up and tries the knob of the outer door. It is unlocked and leads directly on to the street. The three of them get up slowly, look around cautiously, nod to each other and leave. Never sure whether this was an accident or deliberate, they are never bothered again.

Margot gets up to pour herself some brandy and passes the decanter to Beka.

"It was always a mystery as to why he let us go. We came to the conclusion that this officer was a professional soldier. We knew that most of the Wehrmacht did not want to do the dirty work of the Gestapo. I have always been grateful to that man. When we left the Excelsior, we went directly to a friend who was willing to let us stay for a short time. My father returned to our apartment very late that night and packed up our belongings and left the keys on the kitchen table. In the morning we took a bus to Haut de Cagnes, a small hill village on the outskirts of Nice, where we stayed for the duration. It's all a long time ago, but I've never been able to go back to Nice or Vienna. There are some things you cannot forget." She pauses before asking, "Can I get you anything? Are you too warm by the fire?

"No, no I am fine. Oh, my goodness, you were so lucky! How fortunate you were interrogated by a soldier who did not sympathize with his country's insanity and you were spared. What did you eventually do?"

"When France was liberated in 1945, I was nineteen years old. As soon as we could, we moved to Paris. My father was not well and my mother thought he would be taken care of in Paris where the hospitals were better equipped. But he died soon after we arrived. He was still a young man. My mother, never a strong woman, became distracted and depressed and one day walked in front of a trolley. I don't know whether she did that on purpose or whether she wasn't paying attention while crossing the street. Soon after she died, I met a man and got married. He was a handsome Frenchman. I thought we were in love and in the course of a few years we had two daughters. Danielle and Fanny. Margot stops talking and then blurts out. "He died three years ago."

"Oh, I'm sorry" Beka says sincerely. Margot gestures dismissively, as if to erase him.

"Don't be. The truth is he ruined my life. After the children were born, he became verbally abusive and systematically pushed me away—I believe it was because I fulfilled what he considered my purpose; producing children. I wasn't needed anymore. It took me awhile to understand that he was probably gay. He divorced me and demanded custody of our children."

"Really! That's despicable!"

Without responding, Margot continues her story. "Before my husband left me, he urged me to go to Argentina where I had a rich uncle who would undoubtedly take care of me. My uncle, also, your uncle, whose name was Reuben, left Bulgaria for Argentina before the war and became a wealthy man. You see, now that both my parents had died, I had no one. But how could I leave my children? The divorce didn't provide me with an income or visitation rights to see my children. He raised them alone and never remarried. Nor did I."

"Why was that? I can't believe you didn't have the opportunity to marry again?"

"My life didn't accommodate that sort of thing. I was too preoccupied. He won custody of our daughters because he was French and well-to-do. I was a foreigner and had been hospitalized briefly, because of my nerves. Well, that's a nice euphemism for nervous breakdown. I had become severely depressed—and why shouldn't I be? But that's what happened. I lost my children and had no resources at all."

Beka is surprised that Margot can tell her all this in such a matter-of-fact way. She assumes Margot has buried the pent-up emotions she has lived with most of her life. She impulsively starts to reach for Margot to give her a hug, but stops herself, feeling that this gesture might not be welcome.

"I had to find a job but I'd never worked before. I was not brought up to work. The only skill I had was my ability to speak a number of languages, and I didn't know what to do with that. Finally, I found a job as a shop girl in a department store, working behind the cosmetic counter. I sold a lot of cosmetics by making up the faces of customers."

Beka stares at Margot transfixed by her story. Margot sits at the edge of her chair, her back straight and occasionally adds more wood to the fire. Her hands remind her of her mother's and her own. She finds it curious that she has such a fixation on hands. They both have long fingers that are slightly disfigured from arthritis.

"Did you like the job?

Margot looks somewhere beyond Beka. She tells her story, as if she is pulling it out of a place reserved for difficult memories.

"Eventually, but it did take time. I had so much to learn. I became resigned that my life would be spent without my children and I got used to my life in general. Living on a shop girl's salary is quite a dull life. Then something happened. Margot looks at Beka, and with a hint of a smile says,

"I was hired by the House of Chanel!"

"What! Are you kidding me! Your story is beginning to sounds like a tale from Grimms!

"Grimms? Yes, I guess it sort of is. I had unknowingly attracted a man who worked for Chanel. He spotted me while I was working behind the counter at the store. When he learned that I spoke many languages, he recommended me to the House of Chanel and I was hired immediately to be the sales representative for their perfumes. My territory was all of Eastern Europe."

"Really! Now that must have been amazing!"

"Yes and no." While it paid handsomely, it was a lonely life."

Getting up, Margot paces around the room. Staring into the flames, she continues.

"So, that's how I spent my life till a few years ago. I traveled constantly, spending most of my time in drab Eastern European cities where I knew no one. As I mentioned, I was paid very well. That was the compensation for having to live out of a suitcase. I became one of the highest paid women in France at the time and I used most of the money to try and regain custody of my children. It took years and years and all I managed to do was get visitation rights."

Margot's body stiffens and her jaw tightens. Beka can feel the rage still emanating from her.

Margot turns her back to the fire and faces Beka. "I missed all the years of watching my children grow up. I wasn't there to soothe them when they fell. I didn't see them learn to ride a bicycle. I never took them to the beach. I wasn't there when they graduated from school, or when they got married. I was never there! I sent them presents but never got a response. Never even knew what they looked like."

Suddenly Margot's face changes. The heavy atmosphere in the room lightens.

"But you know what? Now I am a grandmother and since the death of their father, my daughters and I have finally gotten to know each other and have become closer. They let me do things for them and I have been able to spend a lot of time with my grandchildren. That has made up a little for not being able to raise my own children. So, in the end, I am alright—I retired with a good pension which allows me to live in this nice place near my children. Of course, I suffer a bit from arthritis in my hands and feet and my blood pressure is too high."

Beka sits back in her chair and begins to relax, realizing her body has been rigid for much of the time Margot's been talking.

"If you simply scratch the surface," Beka muses, "everyone has a story—poignant, harsh, disappointing, but thankfully there is sometimes redemption or a silver lining. For some people, things happen that soften their journey. A gesture by a stranger, a bit of luck." She notices that Margot, over the course of the evening has begun to look more and more like her mother. She, too, must have been a handsome woman.

Beka breaks the mood that has permeated the room and starts to clap.

"Bravo! Bravo! Margot! Let's raise a glass, Here's to you! I find your story remarkable. It's amazing that you found a way to get through this sordid life. It seems if we don't die in the effort, we all find a way to live a life no matter what is thrown at us."

Beka and Margot both start laughing as they lift their glasses and toast each other before settling back and finishing the remains in the decanter.

14

RACHAEL'S LETTER

ALL THE WAY back to Sofia, Beka mulls over what she has learned. Her connections are deepening. She is experiencing a dual feeling of elation as well as sadness, remembering the ever-changing moments of her life and the looming threat of her own mortality. While she has been unearthing the past, she has become even more aware of her own long history. Not knowing when her life will come to an end sometimes scares her, alarmed to realize three-quarters of it may already be gone. But then she is buoyed by this new adventure and grateful for the opportunity to sit down with people who have known a different time and place. It strikes her as a gift she might not have been given had it not been for the apartment she inherited, igniting her interest in this family.

Pondering this on the relatively short flight back to Sofia, she wonders if Michael will be there to greet her, surprised at how much she's missed him and anxious to share what she's been told.

Arriving at her apartment door, she calls out to Michael, but gets no response. The apartment is empty. Putting down her bag she notices a note on the table.

> *"I decided to go on a short trip for a few days. Not sure when I will return, but I won't be long. I'll call.*
>
> *Michael."*

Searching for a corkscrew to open one of the bottles of wine they bought a few days ago, she pours out a glass and looks around. Being alone in the apartment for the first time unnerves her. Throwing a clean bedsheet over the ugly flowered couch, she sits and stares at the room, sipping the wine. It's already three in the afternoon, and while she hasn't had lunch, she's not very hungry. Images of her young parents and her older sister seem to be everywhere and the long-gone ambiance of the elegant pre-war Sofia she lived in after she was born surrounds her like a ghost symphony. Michael's note drops from her hand as she closes her eyes and falls into a deep sleep.

Awakened by a heavy knock at the door, she sits up abruptly, trying to remember where she is. When she opens the door, Mr. Lazarov bows and removes his cap handing her an envelope, speaking in his best English,

"This is special deliver for you. I accept. No one home."

Beka, now fully awake, notices with excitement that it is from Rachael. Anxious to read the contents, she almost grabs it from his hand and hastily thanks Mr. Lazarov who is leaning against the door frame, craning his neck to see inside the apartment, clearly hoping to be invited in.

Beka smiles politely as she slowly begins to close the door.

"Oh, this is very important. If you will excuse me…and …thank you, thank you very much."

Beka takes the wine bottle and her glass, and sits at the dining table and takes out the sheafs of paper.

Dear Beka,

I was very happy to meet you and Mr. Petrov and begin our conversation. I have only told you the beginnings of what I know of Ledicia and her family. Since I am not sure when you will be back, or if you will, I have spent the last few days writing down what has only, up-till-now, been an oral accounting of the family story. It was told to me by my late husband and to him, by his father, so on and so forth. Stay in touch and, if it is your pleasure, share with me anything you are learning as well.

Rachael Avraham

15

BABY REBEKAH

Edirne, Turkey
The year: 1495

*A*YEAR OR MORE *has gone by since Ledicia and Isaiah took their marriage vows. Ledicia finds her new life more than agreeable. She can hardly remember what it was like to be without Isaiah. She has fallen more in love with him each day. He has the wonderful quality of being present, always understanding her moods and needs, willing to share his thoughts and accept hers. In the early morning hours, when fully awake, she loves to lie quietly with Isaiah's arms wrapped around her, or at night when he covers her with his strong body. These are the moments when she feels they are one.*

Taking on the role of the wife of a scholar and rabbi seems to come naturally to her. She often takes over the duty of visiting members of the community to make sure they are well and to listen to their grievances and when possible, advise them. She helps Isaiah with his writing and his sermons. One thing that is important to her, is confessing to Isaiah that she cannot accept some of the teachings or a number of the religious practices of their faith, though she assures him that she is guided by a spiritual, moral, and ethical code. Isaiah, while not in agreement with all her beliefs, respects her ponderings though he questions some of them. Their discussions are quite heated at times. She wonders why God cannot be defined simply by the natural and physical laws of the universe. She questions the practice of anthropomorphizing God. She does not view man as the image of God, but thinks of God as the spirit within man.

They have been married for well over a year when she begins to feel signs of a change in her body. Her breasts have grown larger and she is sometimes sick at odd hours of the day. After three months she is sure and bursts into Isaiah's study to deliver the news. She steps behind his desk, bends down and throws her arms around his shoulders.

"I am carrying the first of our children, my love. We are going to become parents. This is the start of our family."

He gets up from his desk, takes her in his arms, overcome with joy, hugs and swings her around, then stops himself abruptly, fearing that he might damage the child.

"I'm sorry. I shouldn't have done that...here sit down, do you need some water? How are you feeling? What can I get for you? You must rest."

The entire household busily prepares for the first child. Ledicia is happily sewing blankets and clothing. The village woodworker is making a cradle. A room in the house is designated as the nursery and the walls are washed down and painted, the tile floor cleaned and polished.

Her pregnancy goes well and she finds herself in labor right on time. After the fifteenth hour of pushing, breathing and screaming, their first-born arrives, a girl with a full head of dark hair. Ledicia, exhausted, experiences a sense of peace that she can barely describe. Once the baby has been cleaned and swaddled and lies comfortably in her cradle, Ledicia lays her head down in the soft folds of her pillow and goes to sleep. She feels as though she has *just done something miraculous…that out of all the pain has come a perfect gift…Rebekah.*

As the months go by, Ledicia spends much of her time taking care of Rebekah. After a few months, she resumes some of her duties, always taking her baby with her when she makes her visiting rounds. She is often found in the nursery staring at her daughter while she sleeps. Ledicia takes her daughter's little hand and hums a soft lullaby. The baby is thriving. When she gathers her up to nurse her, Rebekah's eyes are now wide open and focus on her mother's face. Her dark hair has become lighter now, her eyes change from a hazy grey/blue to a dark brown. Ledicia is caught off guard by a well of the deepest, clearest, feelings of love and protectiveness she has ever known.

Ledicia wakes up with alarm to see the sun streaming through the window. realizing it is later than usual as the sun is already high in the sky. Last evening, for the first time since Rebekah was born, they entertained a large group of friends and the festivities went on well into the morning hours causing them to oversleep. She rushes into the nursery, surprised that her daughter has not stirred. Usually, it is her early morning cries that wake Ledicia, signaling that she is hungry. As she reaches into the cradle to pick her up, Ledicia discovers that her beautiful baby is lying very still. It takes a few minutes to register what she sees before she screams for Isaiah. He rushes into the nursery to see a sight he will never forget. Ledicia is sitting on the floor moaning, rocking back and forth, holding their dead baby.

Both Isaiah and Ledicia are broken. They feel sure that all the light in their lives has been turned off. All the good things that life once offered, are gone. An emptiness hollows out Ledicia's days. Her sullenness returns. Isaiah is suffering too, but his religion allows him to carry on. Days, weeks and months go by, but the nightmare doesn't fade. The morning discovery of their lifeless child remains a fixed and terrible memory. Even years later Ledicia will be caught by surprise by the image of her lifeless daughter and the morning she disappeared from their lives. She will gasp and stop what she is doing and begin to sob.

What hasn't been broken, what allows them to finally take back their lives, is their devotion to each other. In time, it is the one ingredient that helps them both heal enough to believe they can survive even this. In the years that follow, three children are born to them. Two sons and another

daughter will fill most of the empty place reserved for Rebekah. All of these
children will live.

—

This isn't the end of Rachael's storytelling, but Beka stops to take in
what she has read. Heaving a sigh, she is surprised when she begins to
cry. Was this, she wonders, the first time the name Rebekah was given
to a member of the family? Is her name one that has come down from
hundreds of years to honor a little girl who was never able to grow up?

She wishes there was a painting of Ledicia and Isaiah. She wants to
see them, though she has already drawn their image in her minds-eye.
She knows Ledicia had thick glossy hair and blue eyes. From this she has
invented a picture of her. She feels Ledicia would have been a little more
than medium height and endowed with a strong lovely countenance.
Isaiah, her great grandfather many times over, would be tall, particularly
for those times, and strongly built. He undoubtedly would have had a
long sharp nose, deep-set eyes that were set close together, and high cheek
bones that gave him a look of ascetic intensity and kindness. If she could
paint them, she would dress them in rich dark colors. In the painting
they would be sitting in a forest with a verdant landscape behind them.
Rebekah, their beloved child would be lying on Ledica's lap, a faint white
glow surrounding her. Above all three there would be a translucent angel
just out of reach. She imagines a faint blue aura around all three.

Beka can't stop crying. Baby Rebekah's death haunts her. Tears come
easily to her these days anyway. But there are some things that are harder
to imagine than others. Harder to reconcile. Animals and children in
pain or suffering never fail to upset her, and she cannot imagine anything
more devastating than losing a child. Although this happened over five
centuries ago, Beka feels the loss as strongly as if their loss happened to
her. Taking a sip of wine and composing herself, Beka reads the last line
again. "There were other children born and lived."

"Thank God," she murmurs, and continues to read.

Edirne, Turkey
1497

Naftali, their first son is born two years later. It will be Ledicia's job to rear him when he is very young. The ethical lessons that will make him an asset to this community will be taught by the learned men in the community later. After two years, Armand is born. Two boys will now carry the Avraham name. But there is one more to come. In 1501, Simca, the daughter that Ledicia had so desperately hoped for, is born.

It is to her daughter Simca that Ledicia devotes a good portion of her time. She teaches her to read and write, as her father did for her. In another two years the boys are tutored by Isaiah and other men. As they grow into tall, strong boys, both parents are relieved that their sons take seriously the teachings that are instilled in them. But the boys have very different personalities. Naftali, the eldest, is very sure of himself and a bit bossy. He is also fastidious and organized. Armand is quieter, preferring to spend time drawing and reading and is often forgetful. The older boy has an affinity for weapons. The middle child spends most of his time feeding birds and helping to plant and harvest the vegetable in the garden. Ledicia sees her own features in Simca, and the same strong willful nature she possesses and encourage her, even while she knows it may bring her trouble when she is fully grown. Like Armand, Simca tends to be a more questioning thinker, while Naftali is smart, he rarely sits still and is always boisterously good natured. He, unlike his brother and sister, likes to go hunting with the men in the village.

Though considered radical, Ledicia establishes a school for the girls in her community. Rumors and whispers run through the town. A woman teaching girls is unheard of, but a woman with her ideas about religion and education is worrisome. Her stubborn dedication to her work, and the good results, eventually quiet most of the neighborhood and very few feel they can complain openly. The acceptance of what she is doing is demonstrated by the willingness of enough families to send their daughters to her.

Turkish life is alive with art and culture. The ruler Sulemein is not only sympathetic to a new vision of Turkey but endorses and supports it. In this classical Ottoman period, the Jews along with other communities in the empire enjoy a level of prosperity and congeniality that unfortunately will not last.

One of the difficulties in this otherwise fruitful time is a lack of unity among the Jews themselves. They have come to the Empire from many different countries, bringing their customs and opinions with them and are not willing to give them up easily. This frustrates Ledicia, realizing she is often alone in her thinking and isolated because her ideas are not always welcome. Being wise enough to understand this, she begins to keep her thoughts to herself when in public so that she can continue to teach most of the girls in the community, not only to read and write but to change the culture of how women view themselves.

Isaiah being ahead of his time, though not always in agreement, is proud of his wife. She infuses in her own children, many of the principles she feels strongly about, but at the same time has the generosity to allow them to develop in their own way. She's never been in agreement with the notion that a woman's only role is one of support to one's husband. She is convinced women have been and can be leaders and this is how she tries to comport herself. However, she knows change will come slowly and that she won't always be able to remain either submissive or silent. She must still measure her words and deeds carefully. She has figured out when she should be silent and when to boldly forge ahead.

Knowing he will always have his hands full with Ledicia's stubborn intellect, Isiah loves Ledicia enough to allow her the space she needs. He is proud of how she demonstrates to their children, her independence and love for learning.

Black Plague Doctors of Death

16

THE DEATH OF LEDICIA

RECOVERING FROM THE sad story of baby Rebekah and learning a bit about the other children, Beka turns to the last pages in the packet. Calculating the dates, this part of the story continues some twenty years later. She holds her breath when she sees what Rachael has written.

Edirne, Turkey
September, 1522

Arriving home from the market, Ledicia feels feverish. She lays the basket of vegetables on the wooden table before she loses her strength and collapses.

Isaiah finds her on the cold tiled floor and carries her to their bed. Waking up, she is shivering and asks for another blanket. Isaiah is fearful and asks the house staff not to enter the room. The doctor confirms what Isaiah suspects. She has contracted the Plague. The black death already ravished the city once before and has returned with a vengeance. Everyone thought the Plague had finally petered out, but it has been killing people over much of Europe and Africa.

The city tacks a black cross to the front door of their home, announcing that no one may enter. Food and medicinal herbs are brought to the back door by their neighbors and left for the family. Isaiah believes he is immune because of his own exposure a few years earlier. Having survived he is praying that his beloved Ledicia will be able to survive as well.

He instructs the small staff that he is the only one who can tend to his wife. He employs various herbs, mustard, mint, horseradish and softly ground mashed apples and vinegar baths. as are the remedies of the day, while the doctor comes daily to perform the blood-letting. She shows no signs of improvement, but Isaiah is hopeful because she is still conscious.

"Isaiah, please don't work so hard. I don't think it will help. Just promise me that you will live."

Her voice falters, but she gathers up enough strength to tell him what she fervently does not want him to forget.

"I love you and the children with all my heart. I have…" She stops to catch her breath, and tries to smile as she sees the worried lines on Isaiah's face.

"I have lived well. You have made it possible. I am not afraid of death, but I don't want to leave you and the children, but I think my time has come."

These are the last words she is able to speak. Within a day she begins to bleed from her mouth and nose. Large red blotches appear over her body as blood seeps under her skin. She is no longer conscious but Isaiah never stops talking to her, hoping she can still hear him. On the fourth day, her entire body succumbs to the virus and she goes into shock. She will be spared, at least, the last of the plague's devastating symptoms, gangrene. At age forty-eight, Ledicia is dead.

Isaiah, now a man of 52 sits alone in his study, brooding and praying, as Ledicia is being prepared for burial. He has been in a state of grief that began the day she collapsed, knowing even then that he would lose her.

It is up to him to perform the ritualized ceremony for Ledicia's burial, where she will be laid to rest in the cemetery next to the temple. Both their son's Armand and Naftali are in attendance along with their wives and children. Their unmarried daughter, Simca, is unable to attend, as she has been living with relatives in Amsterdam, helping with household chores in preparation for the birth of her aunt's baby. When able, she has been attending University classes. Because of the exploding Plague, she is not permitted to leave the city.

At the gravesite, Isaiah recites a number of psalms. A ram's horn is blown. Friends of the family take their turn in offering a eulogy, expounding on Ledicia's fine qualities and her many good works. Her sons are the last to speak and simply express their love and remembrances of a mother whose wisdom and good nature continued into their adulthood.

The casket is carried to the burial site and the men in attendance escort her to her final resting place. The act of carrying the casket, in their religion, is thought of as 'Chesed'– the ultimate act of kindness. It is an essential practice, considered a 'Mitzvah', a commandment and a significant good deed because it is something that cannot be repaid.

Had Simca been able to come, she would not have been able to accompany her mother to her grave because women are not allowed to escort the casket. This would offend her as she has grown away from such beliefs and has become a young woman who rejects these arcane rituals. In this way she is quite like her mother.

Ledicia's body is carried with her feet facing forward, but before the casket is lowered to the ground, it is turned so that her head is facing forward while Isaiah repeats a prayer three times, extolling God's compassion. Once they leave the cemetery, everyone in attendance washes their hands three times without drying them.

For the next month Isaiah spends his days in his study or out by the lake where they used to walk daily. They were married for twenty-seven years, *and he is remembering each one. He marvels that neither of them ever took for granted the blessings or the hardships they lived through, but were certain that they were one half of what made them whole. He remembers once again the anguishing moment when they knew their little girl, only a few months old had died in the night. That image has stayed with him all these years. But Ledicia's death is a loss from which he is not sure he will recover, or even wants to.*

Putting down the last of the pages, Beka is once again overcome with grief. Ledicia and Isaiah's story is perhaps the most beautiful one she has heard. There is a feeling of awe that comes over her, knowing that in the long history of her family there was such a beautiful love story. Most of the marriages she has witnessed were made either for convenience, necessity or habit. Rarely had anyone's story risen to this epic level. It reminds her, though not as epic, of the moments and years of her own marriage. A marriage, that surprised her, arriving later in life and one she never thought she would find or deserve.

Beka realizes she's been identifying with Ledicia, though she has never been that brave or smart. This woman that lived so long ago, feels like someone she has always known. Sitting in this apartment in the center of the capitol city of the country where she was born but never lived, she marvels that she has just read a story that has taken her breath away. Beka breaks down and sobs for all the glorious sadness that is part of life.

St George Church - Center of Sofia,Bulgaria

17

MICHAEL RETURNS

TWO DAYS HAVE gone by and Beka hasn't heard from Michael. She spends the first day not leaving the apartment in hopes that he will show up. Knowing she is foolish to worry about Michael's absence, she tries to get in touch with another cousin. When she rings her up, she learns they are away and won't return for another few weeks. Vicki, a first cousin, is the daughter of her mother's brother, born a year after the war ended. She grew up under the thumb of the communist government. Disappointed that she cannot meet her yet, Beka decides to go shopping, but before she does, she visits a square in the center of Sofia where her mother grew up.

The U-shaped square is surrounded by elegant buildings that house the Bulgarian Presidency and the Ministry of Education. The luxurious Sofia Hotel Balkan, constructed in the square in 1956, is a grand fusion of classical design and lavish décor. The iconic building is part of the President's Palace complex and beneath its foundation lies a historic Roman fortress. There is a small red brick church, St. George, built in the 4th century which sits in the middle of the square. Her mother's childhood home, overlooking the square, was bombed by the Americans. Beka still has the address and discovers there is a casino there now. Standing in the center of the square, Beka is amazed that this is what her mother saw every day as a child.

The little 4th century church tempts Beka to go inside. The guidebook says it's the oldest building in Sofia. Entering the church, it takes a while for her eyes to focus as she feels the musty coolness of the rotunda. It suffered some damage during the war but there has been extensive work done to preserve the architecture and the frescoes throughout the central dome. Beka picks up a pamphlet which claims that five layers of frescoes dating as far back as the 6th century, have been restored after they had been painted over during the Ottoman period when the church had been converted into a mosque. The church is built among the ruins of Roman buildings. In front of the church there is an extensive archaeological dig which has unearthed a few of the public buildings, one that even shows a typical hypocaust floor. They have been able to dig up a whole street and a basilica.

Even though there are so many government buildings and ancient ruins on this square, the entire area is an open public space. Eating a grilled chicken sandwich she bought at a local café, Beka sits on a bench that gives her a grand view of the whole area. Observing the activity all around her, she begins to feel perfectly at home.

—

No sooner has she taken off her coat and picked up the bag of groceries to bring to the kitchen, than she hears the front door open. A week has gone by since she returned from Paris and there has been no word from Michael. She greets him cordially, hiding her annoyance. He said he would call and never did. On the other hand, she certainly doesn't want him to feel she has any claim on his private life.

Controlling her response, she calls out, "Hello stranger, I'm about to make supper, are you hungry?"

Michael, oblivious to how his weeklong absence and silence might have disturbed Beka, calls out,

"Yes please, there was no food service on the plane so I can definitely eat. What are you making?" Walking up to Beka, he takes the bag of groceries from her. "Here let me help you with that."

Trying not to make eye contact with Michael, she hopes to mask her annoyance, as she nonchalantly says,

"I hadn't heard from you, so didn't expect you, I was only going to make a salad. I thought it would just be me."

"Whatever you make is fine...any coffee?"

"Yes, I'll put the water on. I'm going to have wine."

"Great, pour me a glass...I'll have coffee after. Just going to wash up."

Beka had been anxious to see Michael when she got back from Paris. She was disappointed that he wasn't there. Now that he is back, she is aware that her mood has suddenly lifted. She notes with some suspicion that he is in very good spirits. Why? Questions begin bubbling up. Where has he been? What has he been doing—and with whom? Confused about what she is feeling, she attempts to control these thoughts and puts a lid on her curiosity. She thinks defiantly that if he wants to share what he has been doing, fine. If not, well then, so be it.

The fact is she's been feeling unsure of herself since returning from Paris. She never minded being alone before, so she is surprised at how much she has missed Michael's company. He does have a way of being very engaging and enthusiastic. It's only this afternoon that she finally began to feel quite peaceful.

Michael returns to the kitchen, with a towel around his neck having just showered and changed into jeans and a sweater. He looks relaxed and rather youthful. Beka pours him a glass of wine and begins cutting up an onion that make her tear-up so that she can barely see. Michael comes over and wipes her eyes with the towel. They stand there looking at each other for a time before he lifts up her chin and gently kisses her. She drops the knife on the counter and slowly puts her arms around his neck, returning his kiss with a passion that surprises her. They begin to laugh, self-consciously, which helps wipe away any pretense about what they have been feeling.

Still smiling, Beka looks away. "I didn't see that coming." Silently, they sip their wine and gather their composure. Minutes go by silently. Michael looks at Beka who returns his gaze, takes Beka's glass placing it on the counter, puts his arm around her and leads her into his bedroom.

It's eight o'clock and dark outside. Beka gets up to find the light switch and hits her knee on the bedpost as she searches for a robe. As she tries to rub the pain away, she calls out.

"Are you still hungry?"

Michael managing to control his laughter, gets out of bed.

"Yes," he says, coming over and begins rubbing her knee. "Hungrier than ever! Do you still want to cook, or shall we go out?"

"I'm happy to stay home and prepare a meal."

In silence, Michael cuts up vegetables and makes a salad while Beka prepares a cabbage stew her mother made often. In no time at all, they have set the table, opened a new bottle of wine, and as they settle at the table, napkins on laps, they pick up their wine, bring their glasses together, focus their eyes on each other, and toast one another.

"So, Michael, let me tell you what I've been doing. My trip to Paris was marvelous. I'll tell you about it later. When I got back, besides not getting to visit my cousin Vicki, I did go to the square in the center of Sofia where my mother grew up."

She precedes to tell him about the church and the archaeological dig, and that she saw a casino where her mother's childhood home had been.

"Michael, I stood in the middle of that square overcome with emotion. I could see the lives of my mother's family going about their day. They are all long gone, yet I could feel them. It was like I was surrounded by their presence. I was sure I could hear them whispering, telling me all about themselves."

Beka stops talking. Clearly, she's trying to divert his attention away from what transpired between them.

Michael clears his throat and puts down his fork. "I bet you are wondering where I've been?"

"I have? Yes, I have."

Beka, afraid to look at Michael, concentrates on cutting her meat. Her imagination runs the gamut of all the possible things he might say. She looks up at him,

"Fine, what do you want to tell me."

Michael explains that he flew to London to visit his children. Then he pauses before continuing.

"I saw my wife."

Beka slowly puts down her knife and fork and sits perfectly still.

"I needed to be sure my wife and I were of the same mind. We've been separated for five years. For all that time I have avoided getting embroiled in any legal business. Not sure why, I just didn't want to. I was very relieved to discover she is in full agreement with what I proposed, and we applied for a divorce."

Beka continues to listen, feeling her face grow hot.

"So, that's what you were doing?" She wants to take a sip of wine but realizes her hands are shaking, so she tucks them on her lap.

"Yes, that's what I've been doing. We've met all the requirements in England. It's not going to be a complicated or a prolonged affair. I was concerned about the children, but they seem to be fully supportive."

"Why did you decide to do this now?"

"It was time, Beka. Long past time. Since I was finally back on this side of the Atlantic. I felt it had to be done. My children are grown and have their own families now. She will, of course, keep the house and take responsibility for it. I have signed it over to her. I don't have to worry about her financially. She is well off and doesn't want anything from me. It has turned out better than expected. Anyway, she's been seeing someone over the last few years, and now she will be free to do whatever she likes...and so will I."

There is another long pause before Beka asks,

"And...you. Do you know what you want to do?"

"I'll stay in the US. I like the University, the students and my job. That's all I'm sure of Beka. He reaches over and takes Beka's hand. As for the rest, it depends, doesn't it? I look forward to finding out."

18

THE WOMAN IN THE PARK

IN THE MORNING Beka slips out of the house to get some air. She needs to think about what happened last evening. At the building's front door, she turns left toward Doctor's Garden Park. On the one hand she feels elated, but hadn't anticipated this would happen and is not sure it's what she wants. She was certain she'd made a firm decision not to become involved with any one after her husband's death: now she's not sure, worried about whether she has any control at all. But she can't deny feeling some of the juice of life returning after years of burying herself in grief.

If it were summer, the trees lining the paths in the park would be shady lanes. Today the branches of the trees are bare and make squirrelly patterns against the sky. Everything is gray and exposed. The air is brisk but not too cold and she pictures this walkway in the summer. Trees on either side of the path will spread their leafy branches, reaching out to each other to make a verdant tunnel.

"I'd like to be here in the summer."

The idea of staying longer had seemed unimaginable just a few weeks ago. But now everything seems possible. She can, if she chooses, stay as long as she likes. There is no compelling reason for her to be anywhere in particular. Being able to make choices is not something she was ever able to do. There was always someone or some reason to do what was expected. She stops walking so she can digest the notion that she is, at this time in life, free to do whatever she wants. It's still quite early in the morning and the park is empty–so she says out loud; "There is nothing to stop me!" And like a young child might, she begins humming words from an old Mamas and Papas song that streams through her mind;

I can do what I wanna' do, go where I wanna' go.

She resumes walking with a lighter step.

After a half-hour, she slows down, relieved to see a pretty gazebo up ahead. A lone woman is sitting on a bench reading the paper so Beka takes a seat on the opposite one. Every once in a while they catch each other's eye, smile shyly and turn away. The woman clears her throat and addresses Beka in Bulgarian. Beka stops her, saying in the only Bulgarian she knows,

"Sŭzhalyavam, che ne govorya bŭlgarski. az sŭm amerikanets." (Sorry I don't speak Bulgarian, I am American.)

The woman smiles and begins to speak in a strong English accent. "I have an extra cup of coffee. It was meant for a friend, but she hasn't shown up. Would you like it?"

"Why yes, thank you, I would. I left the house before I had one. Can I pay you for it?"

" Absolutely not. Please." The woman walks over, sits down next to Beka and hands her the paper cup. The woman stares at Beka. "I haven't seen you here before. Are you visiting?"

"Yes...well, no. The fact is, I am here because I own an apartment just a block away."

"How interesting. Well, welcome to the neighborhood." The woman hesitates and then decides to speak again.

"If I may ask. You said you are an American? How is it that you have an apartment here?" The woman's friendly face allows Beka to open up.

Taking a sip of coffee, she tells the stranger about her purpose in coming here and how she came to be the owner of the apartment. The woman listens attentively. Beka looks directly at her, noticing that she is rather pretty and of an indeterminate age.

"I'm sorry, I should introduce myself. My name is Rebekah Avraham."

The woman looks a bit shocked and begins to laugh. "Now this is a coincidence. My name is Elise Avraham."

"No, really? That's not possible! How can there be so many Avrahams? Do you think...no that's crazy...do you think...we are related?

The two women exchange phone numbers and make plans to meet again. Beka has the uncanny sensation that this meeting was not accidental. She is curious about this woman, and if nothing else, feels they can be friends.

—

Arriving at Elise's apartment a week later, Beka is quick to notice the polished mahogany of old Europe inhabiting all the rooms she can see from the foyer. Elise seems to be at least ten years younger than Beka, and her outspoken, casual manner contradicts the ponderous style of her tidy formal setting. Taking Beka's coat, she flings it on the hall chair and ushers her into the kitchen where she is preparing coffee. The kitchen seems to be the brightest room in the house and the banquette and table in the corner is in front of a large window where there is a big vase of fresh flowers. Elise sets down some cups, plates and a porcelain coffee service, unlike anything Beka has seen before, along with a plate of small bite-size sandwiches. Elise entreats Beka to sit.

"This was my grandmother's apartment. It hasn't changed much, has it? I haven't bothered upgrading it. Actually, I don't want to. I kind of like it the way it is."

"I agree. I like it very much, Elise," looking admiringly at the antiquated stove.

"My Grammy Ruth, left Bulgaria when she got married and moved to Vienna. But during the war she moved to England with her son. That's where I was born. She was an interesting and, I'd say, a strange lady. When the iron curtain fell, she returned to Bulgaria for the first time after all those years, happy to get away from the English weather and the awful food she complained about all the time. She never took to England at all. She lived in this apartment, which belonged to her parents, for a few years, but unexpectedly returned to England where she died a rather sad death. By then she was almost deaf, and the nursing home she was put in was not pleasant at all. After she died…and after my own divorce, I decided to come here to live for a while. I needed to come to terms with the direction my life was going."

"Why did your grandmother go back to England?"

"I suppose because the only family she had left were her son, (my father), and grandchildren, (me and my sister.) Even though she was my grandmother, I was never particularly close to her. Aside from being a strict vegetarian, she was a germaphobe. I remember that she always wore gloves whenever she went out and kept her wild, wiry hair contained in a hairnet. She was always wiping everything down and covered every chair and couch in this house with plastic. The only thing I did was to remove them when I took over the apartment.

She was also picky and demanding. I learned that her husband, (my grandfather), had been a well-off banker who didn't spend very much time at home. He was always busy. They were, I believe, not a happy couple. At the very beginning of the war, my grandmother and her son were evacuated to England from Vienna but my grandfather stayed behind and unfortunately perished in Bergen-Belson.

Beka gasps. "Oh no!"

"I know. It's horrible to think what he must have gone through and though I never knew him, I think about him a lot." Elise pauses before continuing.

"It's hard to know what their married life was like. She avoided talking about it. All I was told was that Elias Avraham, my grandfather, was one of thirteen children born to a wealthy Sephardi family. His mother Blanche, my great grandmother, came from Edirne, Turkey and my great grandfather, Nafatli Avraham came from Ruse. He was from a long line of Avrahams, most of them in the paper business."

The names and places startle Beka. There is something so familiar about them. Beka feels a chill run up her spine, and she begins to shiver. Could it be, she wonders?

Noticing how intently Beka is listening, Elise continues.

"I was told very little about my grandfather, except that he was a quiet distinguished man who together with two of his brothers operated a bank that had branches in Vienna and Paris. And though my grandmother was educated in Germany and lived in Paris for a time, and Vienna for the seven years of her marriage, the only place she was nostalgic for was Bulgaria. Because she rarely spoke about her husband or their marriage, much of what I know was told to me by my father which isn't much. He went missing from my life for many years."

"Where did he go?"

"Ah…well, I'll tell you about that when we get to know each other better. Suffice it to say he wasn't a very honorable man. He did what he thought he had to do, and it wasn't always exactly legal. Anyway, my grandfather's father had a paper business in Ruse, as well as Greece and Turkey. The daily newspapers in all three countries were printed on paper made in the Avraham mills from forests that they owned all across Bulgaria and through Greece and as far as the island of Corfu as well as the outskirts of Istanbul."

Once again, Beka perks up when she hears about the paper business. Her own father, along with his two brothers operated a papermill. Was this all coincidental?

"When Grandmother Ruth did talk, she mostly reminisced about her childhood and seemed almost happy…something she never was. She would go on about her trips to the Black Sea, picnics along the Danube, sledding in the winter, weekends spent in the Vitosha mountains. She reminisced about trips with her best friend, whose father had one of the first cars in Bulgaria. They would drive through the countryside where they picked fruits from the trees. Living in England she planted peach and pear trees in her own backyard. But what I remember most is how often she would instruct us; "Never marry or have children!"

Beka listens carefully to everything Elise is telling her so she can record it later on. "What you've told me, leads me to believe that we may be distant cousins, on your father's side. I'm sure of it. How did we not know about each other?"

Grand Synagogue of Edirne

A village in Bulgaria

19

THE HILLS OF EDIRNE

S TEPPING OUT OF the shower, Michael reaches for a towel and walks into the bedroom.

"I've been thinking, Beka, we should take a vacation!"

"Sooo, I guess this isn't your idea of one?" Beka laughs and looks up at Michael as he enters the bedroom soaking wet. She has been enjoying their new intimacy and Michael's affectionate nature. She does love his spontaneity which is often a contrast to her own practical nature and his occasional sober reflections.

"Hanging around musty buildings, talking to lots of people, taking notes and… well…working is fun, I admit it. It's what we intended to do, but wouldn't it be great to take a trip and visit other countries in Europe.

"Hold on! Isn't that a lot?"

"Not really. We can go wherever you like. Why not spend time in countries we've never been to. Who knows, it might be our last chance. And any way we should find out if…"

Michael stops himself. What he was about to say is: if we are able to spend the rest of our lives together, but knows instinctively that might frighten her.

Beka is pretty sure she knows exactly what he was about to say, and though she would prefer to stick to the research, there is no doubt she would love to spend time traveling with him. The worry is that she may become too dependent on his company. She already lost the man she'd loved for so many years. Between the years of illness and his death, she promised herself she would not go through that again. On the other hand, she sees the benefit of being here and taking a break from their work. It's so tempting to spend time in places she never thought she'd have a chance to see and with such a charming and willing companion. Why not? And didn't she recently accept her newly acquired understanding that she is free to follow her impulse and do what she wants? It's risky though. She hesitates to admit that she may have already fallen a bit in love with Michael. Has he fallen for her? He hasn't really said. What if they don't get along? Will she be disappointed? So far, she can't find any reason to complain. He has been a wonderful companion and lover. But she isn't sure of herself. Relationships can be scary. Not sure she won't find herself clinging to safety. She's never taken rejection very well. She'd hoped to become a woman without obligations or for that matter deep feelings.

"If what, Michael?"

"If…we can keep getting along…you know, caring for each other. There's always a danger we'll begin to quarrel and not trust each other, right?"

Rather than continue the conversation, Beka leaves the room to get a glass of water. When she returns, she's made up her mind.

"Yes. Let's do it! What the hell. But can we afford it? Where should we start?"

"We'll figure it out. It's almost May. Perfect time to travel. Tourists haven't started to arrive. How about Edirne? Some of the origins of your family history started there. We can circle our way across Eastern Europe and come back via Vienna. There are train passes and small hostelries which will certainly make it less expensive, although I'd prefer to rent a car. I mean, we can go any place you like, spend as much time as we like in certain places, as long as we are back here at the beginning of June, when I have to return to the States."

"In June?"

"Yes. I have summer courses I am obliged to teach."

"Yes, of course you do. I forgot." Beka pauses before saying what she's been considering for some time.

"I'm thinking of staying in Bulgaria a while longer."

"You are? Well then, all the more reason to do this now. Edirne, first stop?

"Okay. First stop."

With the enthusiasm of his plan, Beka finds Michael's casual attitude both charming and disconcerting. He doesn't seem bothered that she plans to stay. Maybe this is all just a lark for him. Maybe she should stop overthinking this. Maybe, she needs to lighten up! Why does she always have to make everything so important?

—

They arrive in Edirne, after driving south from Sofia, giving them an opportunity to see a good deal of Bulgaria's countryside. Each mile is a reminder of what her life could have been. She always wondered what it would have been like to grow up in Europe. But for the war, this is where she would have been brought up. Of course, she is grateful that her family came to America when they did. Still, she always thought she would have liked being European.

Driving through sweeping vistas and tiny villages they become aware of how many people here are still conducting life in the old ways. Many villagers still travel by horse and cart. Small tightly packed hamlets are at the edge of acres of hilly terrain and farmland. There is a quaint homeliness to these villages and its people. They have ancient faces, live in dilapidated dwellings that are built alongside the grandness of the surrounding mountains. It feels like they are very slowly, almost in a glacial way, succumbing to the ways of a still distant modern world.

Beka holds out the hope that they will have an opportunity to do some investigating. Michael, while willing, is of a different mind. He wants to take the time to hike the hills. There are small restaurants where they can stop for lunch, or spend hours looking at mosques and town squares. He is happy to observe the people and enjoy the sunset on a deck, with a glass of ouzo, overlooking a lovely landscape, enjoying the fragrance emanating from an array of potted flowers. He'd like to dress for dinner after a day of hiking and sight-seeing. Stay in friendly hostelries, sleep till noon with Beka at his side, have conversations with all kinds of people. They could swim in the Meric River where one can almost see the countries of Turkey, Greece and Bulgaria intersect. Beka is delighted by the lighter side she is witnessing in Michael. But she is still focused on the mission she came here for.

At first glance, they find it interesting to see how much of the ancient city of Edirne has been preserved. There are narrow streets with flowers dangling from balconies. Laundry is strung up on lines between buildings. They find a picturesque hotel in the southernmost part of the city. It's clean, small and pleasantly lively. The river is nearby and there is, or seems to be a mosque around every corner. Edirne has grown and is modern in many quarters, but one also sees country folk driving in with their carts of produce, mingling with the urban habits of the city.

After lunch and a quick nap, they follow a path leading to the outskirts of town and before long there are no more houses, just walking paths up the grassy hillside. Reaching the top of a steep hill, they stop to rest. Michael exhilarated, hugs and impulsively plants kisses all over Beka's face.

"Aren't you glad you agreed to this journey. Isn't it marvelous!"

The rolling hills go on as far as they can see, covered with grass, moss and wildflowers. Some of the land is cultivated with tobacco but the land is used mainly for grazing. Outcroppings of glacial rock formations and groves of olive trees lie along a river that curves its way through the uneven land.

"It looks so peaceful now, as if untouched by all the years of wars and invasions that happened here." They both grow quiet, deep in their own thoughts.

The ghostly sounds Beka begins to hear are the echoes of ancient soldier's boots trampling the gentle shoots of grass to mud, blood soaking into the earth, bodies decaying and binding with the soil. All the ancient wars that have been fought in this region have erased the notion that man ever had the capacity to remain peaceful.

Thrace lies a distance to the right. It's a strip of land she knows is there but not visible from where they sit. It is defined only by an imaginary political border. In its long history it belonged to Greece, at other times to Turkey and for some years to Bulgaria. Today it is part of Greece once again. Ownership always depends on who wins the war on any given day. Country's borders are often made by war, not by natural boundaries. But the land, if it could speak, would say it is not concerned with ownership. It exists, unimpressed by man. It only understands its need for the sun, and the rivers and rain that keep it moist. If it could speak, it would not answer to any name. It is man who defines and names it. Man, who marks it with their language, culture and religion. Man, who foolishly believes he can conquer it and who tries to destroy it. But nature will always win out over the conceit of men.

Michael too has been silent. He looks over this vast terrain. Stepping out of his own thoughts he says out loud:

"Back in the 15th century, everything you see was all part of the Ottoman Empire. The Turks were the current rulers and welcomed the Jews from the Iberian Peninsula, and for centuries, the Jews were integrated and lived in harmony with the rest of the people. There were battles and territory lost to the Russians and the Bulgarians and sometimes won back by the Turks, but it was the Second World War that permanently changed the plight of the Jews. There are hardly any Jews here now. While Bulgaria did not send their Jews to death camps as most countries did, earlier in the war, twenty thousand Thracian Jews, then under Bulgarian rule, were deported by the Nazis, brutalized and finally sent by transport through Vienna to Treblinka in Poland where they were exterminated."

Beka is silent.

These were her people. Their blood was no different from others. They were human beings who breathed the same air, produced children in the same way. They were made of flesh and blood, with feelings, homes, families, professions, skills, knowledge and memories. They were treated worse than livestock before they were finally killed.

Shivering and tearing up, Beka feels what it must have been like to be treated so viciously, starved and dehumanized, lacking food, warmth, their family, and even the ability to privately relieve themselves. They were not able to keep themselves clean, wearing the dirty clothes of a prisoner. What must it have been like to feel the demoralizing horror of being looked at, not as a fellow human being, but as a creature who did not deserve to live?

She shakes off the nightmare of her thoughts, almost apologetic that but for the grace of God or whatever higher power there is, she was allowed to live, never having to witness first hand, man's brutal inhumanity.

Michael observes Beka's face as it turns from a delighted sunny spectator of this landscape, to an ashen color. Her face is bent down and twisted.

"What is it?"

"Nothing…well everything. I'm okay. This place brings up thoughts that are hard."

"Yes, it does. Even if one is not a Jew."

"And you are not, are you Michael?"

"No, I was born into the Russian Orthodox religion, but I am an agnostic."

"Me too. Or at least I was."

Getting up they head back to town. Michael takes Beka's hand to guide her down the uneven path, squeezing it from time to time, trying in this small way to reassure her that while life isn't fair or safe, he would like to protect her and take the rest of their life's journey together.

—

Of the thirteen destroyed by fire in 1905, only one synagogue remains. The Grand Synagogue of Edirne was resurrected a year after the big fire. But when the entire Jewish community left the city in 1983 for Israel, Europe and North America, the Grand Synagogue was abandoned. Eventually the roof collapsed along with one of the main walls. It was restored by the Turkish government and reopened just months ago. Beka wants to see it, hoping that some archival documents may have been salvaged.

Walking through the main doors of the Synagogue, noticing the brightness and cheerfulness of its yellow facade, they are impressed by the majesty of the hall and the elegant simplicity of the main part of the temple. They phoned ahead and are met by a rabbinical historian. Beka is keen to find out if there is any trace of Isaiah Avraham and his family in the historical archives stowed away in the underground vaults of this temple. Is it possible that something might have been salvaged from the fire? They are ushered into a pristine room that feels like a sanctuary and are given the time to look over the documents that have been carefully preserved. After a few hours, Beka notices that one of the side walls has a door that leads to a small room in which there are shelves on all three sides. On the shelves are wooden boxes each labeled by year and region. In one of these boxes, she miraculously uncovers a very old bible. Neither Beka nor Michael can read Ladino, but can make out names and dates. It's possible that it is Isaiah's. They need a translator. Told that there is an elderly Sephardic rabbi still living in Istanbul, they rush to call him and coerce him to travel the two and half hours to Edirne with the promise of a donation to his temple and travel expenses.

Beka cannot believe she is holding Isaiah Avraham's ancient bible in her hand. The rabbi has come and gone, but not before identifying that the bible did belong to Isaiah Avraham! The back pages, given for this purpose, hold the dates of births, marriages, death and taxes levied as far back as the 16th Century. Stuck among the pages of the Psalms, Exodus and the Book of Daniel, are loose sheets of paper, written by Isaiah himself. These turn out to be notes for sermons. The Bible seems to grow heavier as Beka feels its ancient weight. She is holding the beginnings of her known world. To hold it is so mystical that she remains speechless, almost transported. On the crumbling parchment papers inserted in this old bible, written in ink that is still legible and pressed heavily on each page, lies the skeletal history of the Avraham family. Once again, proof that there existed a woman who wrote poetry, and the man who loved her. That man presided over the same community for years after her death. They sired four children. One died just months after her birth. Dates confirm when his two sons left Edirne for Ruschuk, and include the dates of their marriages, children's births, and their deaths. There is an entry written of the marriage of Simca, the daughter, and the date of Ledicia and Isaiah's death. Clearly the bible was updated by a Rabbi, after Isaiah's death, who took his place. Beka notes that of the early Avrahams, none lived past their 60th year.

Leaving Edirne with a photograph of the bible and photocopies of Isaiah's notes and the log at the back of the bible, they have a sense that their accidental find is something akin to luck or magic.

When they move on to Crete, they are in a holiday mood. In checking the guidebooks, they decide to stay in the city of Chania for a few days because of the lovely architecture, beautiful beaches, the mountains, and lively nightlife. Finding accommodations in the old town, they spend their first day walking aimlessly throughout the ancient walled Venetian city. In their wanderings, Beka notices a synagogue. It looks quite old, but has recently been restored. Outside the door of the sanctuary's south wall, there is a memorial to the members of the Cretan Jewish community who perished during the Shoah. The names of the victims are listed on bronze plaques, reminding Beka once again of what should never be forgotten.

Coming upon a very old church, Beka lights a candle, her old practice, started years ago. A nod to her acceptance of the unknowable. The possibility that one simple act might have a positive outcome.

By the end of the day, they are eating fresh fish at a local bar near the port, drinking and dancing with the locals.

The next day they take a ferry to Balos beach. Sitting on the pristine white sand they are mesmerized by the crystal-clear water. They marvel that they are very nearly alone. While it is too cold to swim, they run through the water as it laps up onto the beach and find a dune that gives them the privacy to feel safe enough to make love. Beka feels the shadow of years fall away and a lightness that makes her feel as she did in her youth.

Their journey around Europe feels as if the pressure of time does not exist. They are both at ease sharing experiences together. Beka surrenders to the feeling that Michael has become a person that matters very much to her. They are delighted that they have a similar rhythm and like all the same things. It is hard for her to believe she is having all these exquisite moments she thought she'd given up.

In Vienna, their last stop before returning to Bulgaria, Beka once again encounters the tragedy of the War inflicted on members of her family. What is so bewildering is that her parents never talked about any of this.

In the archives at the University of Vienna, Beka finds listed, Carl Avraham, a student enrolled in his sixth semester, studying Philology and Art History. He apparently leaves for Greece, after the summer semester of 1938, where he is also a citizen. Further down the document, there is mention of his mother, Bella Avraham. It reads that she was sent to Maly Trostenet in Belarus in 1941. Nothing further is mentioned except that she died in 1942. Beka knows that Maly Trostenet was the location of a Nazi extermination camp. Bella was her father's aunt and Carl, therefore, his cousin. The listing mentions Carl's father as living in Vienna, originally from Ruschuk. There is no further information about him except that his birth date shows that he was eleven years older than his wife, Bella. Perhaps he had already died before the war. But there is no mention of how or where he died.

Once again, she is confronted with the realities of that war, heartbreaking enough, but now she knows there were people in her family unknown to her, that were exterminated by the Nazis. This information becomes even more personally devastating. This cursory information leads her to ask so many questions. Why did Carl not finish school? It wasn't clear in 1938 that Hitler would cause so much misery. What made Carl leave for Greece, and why did his mother stay in Vienna? Did he suspect the worst? And if so, why did he not implore his mother to leave when he did? Perhaps he did. Maybe she stubbornly refused to leave her home, nor suspecting what was in store for her. Again, more questions than answers.

There is an address in Vienna where the family lived. Beka and Michael go in search of that street. They find a short street sandwiched between two wide boulevards. The Danube International School takes up the full length on the opposite side of that street. Across and at the end of the street is a six-story building. It seems to have been modernized. It looks out onto a wide tree-lined boulevard. The family must have lived quite comfortably here, before the war.

In an attempt to change Beka's mood, Michael suggests they take a long walk in nearby Stadpark and clear their heads. He doesn't want to lose their holiday spirit and suggests they treat themselves to a room at the famous Sacher Hotel facing the Vienna State Opera. Since they are here, Beka concedes to Michael's suggestion that they attend the opera, and for the first time, she enjoys all three acts of Turandot. Their late dinner at the hotel ends with a slice of Sacher-torte, the dessert made famous by this hotel and Beka's not-so-secret pleasure. That night in their imperial red room, they make love in a plush ornate bed, where Michael finally whispers in her ear that he is in love with her. It has been a day of considerable luxury, and at long last, the words she hoped to hear. Beka is grateful for everything, yet she isn't able to forget what happened here so many years ago.

At breakfast, sitting on the balcony overlooking this beautiful city, Beka experiences a moment of anxiety. Their vacation is almost over, and tomorrow they will be back in Sofia. Michael will pack hurriedly and leave for America and she will be alone.

20

IS THERE MORE

ENTERING THE AIRPORT, the first thing they notice is that the air conditioning isn't working and it is packed with people. This confirms Beka's absolute dislike of airports. Her stomach has become familiar with the anxiety that is always present, whether she is going somewhere, picking someone up or saying goodbye.

Walking towards the security gate where they will say goodbye, all she can hear, aside from her stomach, is the sound of their own footsteps. Looking up at Michael, his face shows signs of strain. Beka sees a strand of hair fall on his wet forehead. Patting his hair back, Beka mumbles, "Michael, I don't like airports. Saying goodbye to you here makes me even sadder. I hate it. You will keep in touch?"

"What do you think, silly? Of course, I will." He is a little distracted, fumbling in his jacket pocket for his passport and boarding pass. As his fingers find what he is looking for, he stops and turns his attention back to Beka.

"After all, I'll want to know what you're up to, won't I? All alone in the city." He taps her gently on the nose.

"Really? Don't worry about me," she says stoically. "Besides the city is beginning to feel a little more like home…but I can't stay here forever. I know that. I just have to be here a while longer. Not sure what exactly I will do, but I need to uncover more. I think I'll spend most of my time in Sofia, and work from there. Maybe a few side trips. Not really sure, but I'll figure it out."

Locked in a long embrace, Michael can't see her tears, nor can Beka see the concern and affection on Michael's face. It's hard to let go.

As Michael releases Beka, he brushes his hand against her cheek and kisses her softly. "Yes, yes, we will write often and we will talk. We will stay in touch until you return." Beka nods, trying hard to act nonchalant, but inwardly she is full of doubt. She can't explain her feelings in this moment, but she sees before her a cavernous empty space and she can't help wondering if their relationship will survive this separation. Is she sure she wants it to? Yes, she needs it to. But she knows she isn't ready to leave, which is why she bravely extended her visa for another year.

Slowly disappearing past the security line, Michael's figure melts into the crowd. Beka stands still, planted there long after there is any sign of him. Turning away, she walks slowly towards the exit, feeling very alone. Pushing through the exit door, she thinks, "Dammit, this is my search after all."

These months have been an amazing adventure and she loved spending so much time with Michael, but while she is aware of how much she will miss him, she admits to the beginning tinge of excitement. Being alone in the middle of this foreign city is mysterious and she knows she is going to discover something new. This thought holds her hostage. It is her quest and she needs to celebrate it.

—

Weeks have gone by quickly since his departure and they have kept in touch almost every day. She has begun to enjoy living in the apartment and even bought a few house plants to bring some more life into the rooms. Feeling closer to her parents than she ever did when they were alive, she often finds herself chatting with them, sharing everything that she's been learning. Asking questions about people and places that have no answers, still wondering if they can hear her. If they even know she's here. Maybe one of these days, they will surprise her and whisper back to her. Reveal more of themselves. What, dear parents, did you think about? Did you have many secrets? What made you happy? Did you love us? Did you approve of us? So many questions they could have answered had she asked. The main question is why it has taken her so long to care about the answers. Why does she feel everything she is doing is for the last time? But what is time? Time passes and rearranges us. But by the time we have experienced something, it has already changed. The present moment is all that is real when you think about it. Why is she so interested in what already happened? The more she learns, the more she realizes how each moment that once existed is imprinted in some unknown way into the whole of the universe and is not replaceable.

So, is life only what has not yet happened? Or is life what we are looking forward to? If so, when we experience a moment, has it either just arrived from what was about to happen, so that when that moment passes, does it no longer exist? Is that why we need memories? In our memory, time is fixed. So, is time only a memory? Perhaps time should only be considered the moment it happens, because the present was the future just a while ago.

This morning, the rain has emptied the streets of people. Sprays of water rise whenever a car drives through the puddles forming in the deeply rutted street. Though its early morning the sky looks like charcoal and the scene outside her window is gloomy. Yet, Beka feels marvelously alive. She loves rainy days and stands by the window enjoying the filmy grayness of the day. These days are often spent talking to herself.

When we are young, or certainly when I was, I always thought about what it would be like to be a grownup, as if being a child was not real; that it was merely a springboard for what comes next. But I never thought I would die. Life had an endless supply of days. I think youth is like that. There are a lot of empty patches of time you can't account for, but it doesn't seem to matter, because there are so many more. While I have forgotten those patches and do not know how they affected me; are they still part of me? It has taken me a long time to realize that my birth on that wintry day in January was not random. There are links and chains that connect us to ourselves and to others.

Her mood shifts suddenly. She starts to feel much older. It's a shock to realize she is no longer in tune with the times. She'd always prided herself on her hipness. But many things have changed and she should own up to the reality that she is no longer in touch with the current culture. She does not like the music that is popular today. Younger generations are designing the world she still lives in. It's hard to stay current with the fast-changing culture, artificial intelligence and the digital world. Maybe not for the first time, but in much sharper focus, she mulls over the notion that this is how it must have been for the generation before hers and the generation before theirs. Each generation has to make way for the next one coming. The elders are the stepstones that the younger generation use, but eventually their power withers and they become less and less relevant.

She sinks into a chair, noting how a mild melancholy has washed over her and underscores the fact that her time on earth is already coming to an end. Maybe not right away, but now it's more certain. All the things that were familiar to her are merely quaint notions to the younger generations. She is keenly aware that she is mortal, something she hadn't really considered before. Right now, she feels annoyed with herself for her easy ability to put off things for another day. She finds herself mourning all the things that will never be.

"I'll never be a gymnast, or get a PhD. I won't get to see the gorillas of Rwanda. I wanted to live in New Zealand, for at least a year. That's out of the question. I've put off a lot of things for another time, always thinking I had more of it."

Being alone has given her so much to reflect upon. So much to celebrate. A lot to cry about. She has discovered she is a member of an old family. They lived many different kinds of lives. Opulent and privileged for some. But even they had their share of fear, courageous moments, tedium, joy and pain. The branches of her family tree spread far and wide, heavily laden with life's bittersweet fruit. Now most are only particles of dust that float around the universe. Did those who escaped the hardship and misery of war wonder why they were the lucky ones? Disconnected through sheer self-centeredness, she grew up in America, figuring her own life was enough to conquer. Every one of the lives she is learning about were so different than her own, and yet she can't help feeling that her life has been a composite of theirs. And their history, connected to hers.

Since Michael left, she hasn't been able to uncover many more clues about her family's earliest years. The threads that have been pulled so far have led her back to the 16th century which intrigue her. Ledicia is a woman she has come to admire, even identify with. Isaiah is a man she would have liked to know. What happened to their daughter? Somehow, Beka has a feeling Simca was special. What happened to their sons once they moved to Ruschuk (Ruse as it is called today.) Did what they become provide a link to what her own father and other members of the family would do in their time. Her new acquaintance and possible cousin, Elise, provided her with a few clues. Her own father and his brothers owned a paper mill. How interesting that making paper out of the surrounding forests led to the printing of newspapers. And that newspapers became the way of communicating and that at least one of her uncles was a journalist. Connections and links. She'd like to know more.

There has been a full week of rain. Even Beka has become weary of it. Waking up very early this morning the sun has finally come out. Impulsively she decides to rent a car and drive to Ruse to spend time with Rachael. It is warm now and summer is in full leaf. The Bulgarian countryside is splendid in its rolling coat of green. Beka finds herself singing softly, feeling lighter than she has in days.

As she enters the city, she drives directly to the same hotel she stayed in when she first visited the city. It feels familiar now. Stepping into the lobby of the hotel she is flooded with thoughts of Michael. She hears his voice so clearly that she looks around to see if he is behind her. Disappointed that he is not, she is more aware than ever of how much she misses him.

Finding a place to park a block away from Rachael's apartment, she walks the rest of the way. Rachael is standing in front of her building looking flamboyant in a lightly patterned skirt, wearing a floppy straw hat, no longer resembling the street antique dealer at all. Another thing to ponder. How deceiving first impressions sometimes are.

"Hello Beka. It's such a nice day I thought I'd wait for you outside. Let's go to my favorite bistro. It's just a few blocks away."

Without waiting for an answer, Rachael starts walking confidently down the street, her sandals clacking rhythmically on the concrete side-walk. Beka speeds up and falls in beside her and Rachael locks arms with her as they walk briskly down the street in friendly silence. When they reach the café, Beka is not surprised at how warmly Rachael is greeted by the staff and ushered into the back garden as if it was her private salon.

They sit under the shade of an umbrella helping to cool them from the hot Balkan sun.

Beka notes that the walter doesn't write down her order. He seems to know exactly what Rachael wants, and to make it easy, Beka orders the same thing. Their conversation starts slowly. Rachael asks the usual questions. "How was the drive? Where is Michael? Are you enjoying your stay?" But before long, Rachael is fully engaged in telling Beka more about herself.

"Let me give you a better understanding of where I fit in to our family. I married one of your Austrian cousins who fled the city during the war. Some in that family stayed behind unfortunately—not a good idea at all. I don't have to tell you what happened to them. You can imagine. My husband's immediate family left Austria as soon as they could. They returned to Bulgaria and were among the Jews that left for Israel during the 1948 Exodus. Bastien and his brother stayed behind in Bulgaria. I think, but am not sure, that I am your second cousin through marriage, but I have a hard time getting through all that genealogy. Maybe I am a second cousin twice or three times removed...who knows about these things?

"Not me! I can't help you. I become hopelessly lost trying to figure out how we are all connected, and what names are given to our status. So, you are a relative through marriage?"

"Well not exactly. I am related by blood as well. I'll explain. But welcome to the Avraham club." Rachael laughs and twists one of the rings on her finger, as it has grown a little tight.

Here is how we are related. My husband and I were cousins. His father and my grandfather were cousins...something like that. Bastein was much older than me. Initially he became my benefactor and treated me as a daughter. In time we became closer. I was born in Bulgaria which is where we met at family gatherings during the holidays, but then I left to go to school in Paris where I continued to study dance. I was not having much success finding work. Still, I persevered taking classes and odd jobs whenever I could. I lived frugally, in a small studio apartment and often didn't have enough money for decent food. When Bastien's wife died, he was extremely heartbroken and began to visit Paris frequently.

It was his way of taking his mind off his sorrow. He would meet me and take me to dinner, and after a short while decided to provide me with a monthly stipend so that I could pursue dancing without the strain of having to find jobs that were time-consuming and often menial. Because I could focus on dance, I eventually became part of the corps de ballet of a small ballet company. There was a thirty-year difference in our age, but over time we fell in love and married, much to the chagrin of the rest of the family." Rachael takes a breath and looks questioningly at Beka.

"Does that shock you, Beka?"

"No! I'm not shocked. Really, I'm not! Well, maybe a little surprised." Beka leans over to Rachael, full of admiration.

"But what really impresses me is that you were a dancer. I'm going to admit something. I had dreams of becoming a ballet dancer when I was young. But obviously that never happened. For one thing, I was not built to be a ballet dancer and, anyway, my parents would have none of it."

Rachael smiles and nods. "Well, what did you do?"

"Oh, I did a lot of different things. I often call myself an auto-di-dactic dilettante. But hey, please go on."

"Alright, but I will want you to explain what you mean and what you have done."

"I will, I promise. But now I want to hear your story. Don't lose your train of thought."

"It was my husband, Bastein, who told me Ledicia's story. He did that before he died a number of years ago. When he became gravely ill, he gave me Ledicia's pouch and her book of poems and for days told me parts of the Avraham story. By the time it reached him, I feel sure some of it had become embellished or just plain folklore. But in the main it's true. He was entrusted to carry on the story because he was the youngest son in the family and was likely to live the longest. Shortly after he told me all he knew, he died. There is no one left, so I am the bearer of the story, and now you will be too."

"He was a good man, much younger in spirit than his years. Vigorous too. Then one day he became ill and simply was unable to recover. He continued to take care of me even after his death by leaving me a small inheritance. Consequently, I was able to continue my career. I danced with a small company, touring Europe, until I got too old. When I quit dancing, I worked as a choreographer and started my antique business—which is really more of a hobby."

Beka is amazed and gathers up her thoughts. "How fortunate that you two were able to have as many years together as you had." Rachael nods and for the first time looks a little vulnerable.

Fascinated, Beka hopes there may be more stories that Bastein told her, but the conversation stalls. Beka waits, hoping there is more, but Rachael is wistfully staring into space.

Beka needing to keep the conversation going, brings up the news that she found Isaiah's bible on their trip to Edirne. Hearing this, Rachael perks up, her eyes widen and it is clear she is now actively engaged.

"You did? That is incredible. Are you sure? Do you have it with you? May I see it?"

"No, we couldn't take it out of the archives, but I made photocopies." Beka pulls them out of her large purse and hands them to Rachael. "These are copies from the back of the bible. Here, these are for you. See there is a notation that Isaiah's sons moved to Ruschuk and built a paper mill. There is mention of Isaiah's daughter, Simca, but she has another surname...West?" Do you know anything more about them?

Rachael handles the pages with reverence, reading everything slowly. It's only been a few minutes, but Beka feels like time has stopped as she waits for Rachael's answer.

Looking up at long last, Rachael smiles. "Indeed, I do."

The new paper mill

21

PAPER-MAKING AND NEWS SHEETS

Ruschuk, Bulgaria
September, 1523

*I*T HAS TAKEN *a few years before the Avraham brothers feel they can leave Edirne. Concerned about their father, they have put off a business deal that has been brewing for a few years. Now that their father has come through the darkest part of his grieving and knowing their sister will be staying with him, Naftali and Armand prepare to leave Turkey for Bulgaria.*

When the brothers reach Ruschuk, they find places to live for their family near to the building site of the new paper mill which is in the first stage of construction. Once settled. they are both engaged in making sure the mill is constructed exactly as detailed in the plans from their German partners.

While the mill is under construction, they set about to find some men who they will teach the skills to run the mill machinery and make the paper.

At the same time, Naftali and Armand are also hard at work making sure that they are fully acquainted with the business they are now engaged in. Their partners are men who are financing this enterprise but will remain in their own country and rely on the brothers to set up the business.

Naftali is most concerned about identifying the customers needed to buy their stock once they are producing the paper, while Armand is engaged in finding the raw materials that will feed the mill. Their separate concerns suit them. Armand much prefers being out-of-doors, while Naftali enjoys engaging with people, and developing the legal and accounting practices for the business. The brothers have somewhat different visions for this business. Naftali is concerned with the prospect for making a good living simply by the sale of paper, while Armand dreams of creating a second arm of the business—printing as well as establishing some sort of newspaper.

Acres of woodland is being tapped for sale, and Armand, travels throughout the region, buying up as much forest land as he can.

The business grows substantially in the next years as they become one of the main sources for paper in the region and soon begin to distribute throughout Europe. As the business prospers, the two silent partners make a move to take over the mill from the Avrahams, secretly wanting to cut the brothers out of the business entirely.

Armand has no heart for these conflicts, and nervously spends his days fishing or examining a forest stand of trees. But Naftali is a shrewd and somewhat cunning business man, and relishes the battle he is about to wage.

Without the silent partners knowing it, Naftali had, years ago, applied and received a special patent for the type of millwork they are doing. He made sure the patent was only in the brothers' names. If the partners try to take over the business, they will be forced to pay the brothers a huge sum for the rights to the machinery and the patent. Armand purchased most of the forest land by personally borrowing from a bank. So, the land does not belong to the company. Not only that, but Naftali makes sure that the men he trained will not stay if the business changes hands. The skills required to man the Mill's machinery takes months of training. Purchasing the patent will be difficult if not impossible and the wood to supply the mill belongs to Armand, because when he secured a loan from the bank, he did so in his own name and was able to personally pay-off the debt, so now the forests belong exclusively to him.

It takes a few more years, but eventually Armand tires of the business and becomes more interested in painting and writing. Naftali's sons, now grown, begin to work for their father, assuring that the business will stay in the family.

Armand returns to the business, setting his energy towards his original dream of printing and producing a newspaper. He builds a small printing press in one of the rooms at the back of the mill. Interested in the world outside of his small community, he starts a weekly news sheet that can be distributed fairly cheaply. The newsletter contains local news bulletins, local gossip, and special events. It also contains news of kings and treaties, epidemics and accounts of battles in other parts of the world. He is particularly interested in the effect the Ottoman Empire is having on the surrounding countries. Feeling strongly the importance for the citizenry to know what is going on beyond their city, he begins to report on the various places the Ottoman Empire have already taken over, and the ones in the future it will attack. He warns that the fighting Ottoman forces will likely call upon all the young men in the community to join in these battles. He writes about the takeover of Belgrade, Croatia and Rhodes. He continues to write about the Empire and how it is becoming the largest presence in all of Eastern Europe. While the Empire has been merciful to the Jews, he is often fearful of their reputation as brutal dictators.

22

ISAIAH, SIMCA, EDWARD

Edirne, Turkey & Cornwall, England
The years: 1523-1526

A YEAR IN DARKNESS *has taken the place of the happy and optimistic disposition Isaiah previously possessed. Slowly he begins to resume his duties with more interest and even more empathy than he possessed before.*

His daughter, Simca, studying in Amsterdam, has returned home to be with him. Isaiah's sons' Naftali and Armand, have been given an opportunity to build a paper mill in Ruschuk, Bulgaria. They only leave Turkey when they feel their father has regained his equilibrium.

Printing is an old family skill, taught to them by Isaiah's father who brought the printing press to Turkey from Spain. This was one among many reasons the Empire welcomed the refugees from the Iberian Peninsula. Now, the Avraham brothers plan to bring printing to Bulgaria and make the paper to feed it.

This morning, Simca is sitting at her father's desk reading his latest sermon. Noticing that it has strayed from his earlier ideas, she is delighted to read that he is now less focused on the traditional teachings of the Hebrew scholars, and bends more towards her mother's notion of a humanistic community. He has begun to believe there are good reasons not to hold onto the stagnant ideas of their religion, but to see it as a more fluid and harmonious intersection of faith and the need for daily acts of kindness. Simca has always favored her mother's vision—that this should be a fundamental theme that if carried out faithfully would connect all religions.

The loss of his wife has changed him in a variety of ways. Lately he has begun to feel his mortality more acutely. While his work, once again, becomes important to him, he takes a keen interest in nature, spending hours in the forest outside the city, sometimes writing addresses to the congregation on Saturday mornings, not about a section of the Torah, but about the beauty and necessity of trees.

He also spends a lot of time thinking about Simca, desiring above all else that she get married. He worries that she will be left adrift when he dies. Now fully grown, and at twenty-two almost past the age of marriage, he deeply desires that she reconsider her obstinacy about not accepting any man's proposal.

"I am not interested in marriage, father. I will be fine. My desire is to remain beside you and do the scholarly work that you have started. I do not see children in my future. Please be content that your sons have given you grandsons, and the three of them will pass on your name."

"It is hard to be a woman without the sanctuary of a husband, Simca. I will not be here forever. How can I not worry about you?"

Simca leaves the room, frustrated that she is making her father unhappy and that as a woman has little opportunity to earn her own living and must be beholden to her family or a husband. Needing some air and exercise she walks out into the bright sunshine of this pleasant autumn day. Passing a group of shops, she stops and looks into each one of their windows. She notices a pair of beautiful boots in one shop and looks at her own which she has been wearing for years. But vanity is not a trait that Simca possesses. Not realizing it, she has wandered into a remote part of town. Wrapping her shawl around her head to avoid being fully seen by the cluster of men that are gathered along the road, she is keenly aware that being a woman alone on such a street can be dangerous, particularly as she is not a Christian. Bowing her head, she passes a rowdy group of men who begin to taunt her.

She rushes ahead and goes into the next shop to avoid them. The shop is poorly lit and appears to be empty of people. As her eyes acclimate to the room, she sees that she has entered a print and book shop. She begins to browse and soon loses herself in the bounty of literature before her. Looking up she is startled by a young man that appears from nowhere.

"Are you looking for something in particular?" She cannot see him clearly, but is taken by his beautiful voice.

Trying to come up with an answer she blurts out, "My father needs some parchment paper. Do you sell paper?" As he comes closer, Simca is surprised by his good looks.

"Yes, of course. How much does he need?"

Buying a ream, she is reluctant to leave the shop. The gentleman asks her why she seems so interested in the books on his shelves.

"I can't imagine that you can read them, can you?"

Simca is not sure how to answer this, but finally decides to let him know that she can read and does so often.

"Well, then, let me help you. What is your interest?"

"Philosophy…religion and stories—good stories."

He scans the shelves pulling out a few books. How about Dante's Divine Comedy *or perhaps, Desiderius Erasmus,* The Praise of Folly. *Here,* The Chivalric Romance *by deGaula, or maybe Herodotus's* History *would interest you. He lays them all out on a table. She wants to purchase them all. So far, no one has entered the shop and Simca and the bookseller find a great deal to say to each other. She discovers he is not Turkish as she had assumed, but English. He tells her he arrived in this country as a student.*

"I came to study language and philosophy. Unfortunately, I ran out of money. My family has not been supportive of my interests so I had to stop my studies, needing to earn enough money to return home, though I am not sure where home is for me these days."

Their eyes meet a number of times during their conversation. Each time they do, Simca finds herself blushing…and he has not taken his eyes away. She is lost in the expressiveness of his mouth. Finally she buys The Chivralic Romances, *happy that she studied English while in Amsterdam. When she feels she can stay no longer, she makes a move to leave, but hesitates, then impulsively invites him to dinner the following evening.*

"You will have much to talk about with my father." She hands him her card.

"I am honored to meet you, Simca Avraham, and by your kind invitation. My name is Edward West."

As Simca heads for the door, Edward grabs his coat and locks the door to the shop, after she is on the street, "Let me walk with you as far as the crossroad. It is not safe for a young woman to be alone on this road."

"Thank you, that's kind of you."

She tries to hide her nervousness as they walk together. Approaching the road which turns back towards her neighborhood, she says as formally as she can,

"Good day Mr. West, I look forward to seeing you tomorrow. Six o'clock."

Walking back home, unaware of how widely she is smiling, she wonders what has come over her. What has she done? She has invited a stranger to dinner! How did she become so forward and how can she explain her attraction to this man? He is English and his father is a Baron. Does that make Edward West, a Baron-in-waiting, she wonders, as her mood turns silly.

—

When she hears the doorbell ring, she rushes to open it, greeting Mr. West as if she were the butler. She directs him to the sitting room. Isaiah gets up from behind his writing desk and greets him warmly, though somewhat curious to see that Mr. West is surely not a man from the community. At first the evening proceeds at a polite and somewhat awkward distance, but after the meal is done, a lively conversation begins and continues well into the night. The Rabbi is impressed with the quality of this young man's thinking, and Simca is unabashedly charmed. She has never met anyone like him. He is worldly, yet humble.

Edward had hoped to return to England within the year, but now wants to prolong his stay. Though he is basically a reserved man, he begins to court Simca aggressively, and before long the two are spending all their spare time together.

His stay in Edirne must come to an end and he will be forced to return to England in a matter of weeks. He cannot leave her behind and so asks Simca to marry him. They both know there will be great hurdles to overcome. Both his family and her family will most assuredly object. But they are both very independent people and realize they have no choice but to spend their lives together.

Isaiah upon hearing of the proposal is not happy.

"Simca, I love you dearly and want you to be happy. Mr. West is a fine man, but you must understand that venturing into this territory will be hard. You will be ostracized by both communities. You must think seriously about this. You cannot only follow your heart."

At the same time, Isaiah is trying to understand his own conflicted emotions. He wants Simca to be happy but fears for his daughter's well-being, and cannot reject his own responsibilities.

"Please father. I need your good will. I need your approval. You know that I have never been religious. My mother and I had similar values. Please give me your blessings. I am strong enough to do this and I know Edward is as well."

Torn between the love of his daughter and the allegiance to his people and his religion, Isaiah lives in a state of conflict. He is having difficulty accepting this proposed marriage, although the fact is, since Ledicia's death, he has become more unsure, less doctrinaire about the teachings he is duty-bound to practice. Still, it is impossible for him to bend.

Without her father's blessing or the sanction of the Temple, Simca and Edward are unable to marry in either the temple or the church. They leave Turkey together, but before they do, handfast, by asking friends to be their witness by hearing both of them plight their troth to each other. This action has the legal effect of binding them to each other as man and wife.

Before leaving, Simca hugs her father. Saying goodbye is difficult. They are both in tears. Leaving Edirne they travel to England, where they choose Cornwall to settle, as it is far enough away from Scotland where his family seat resides.

Edward West, the youngest son of the 3rd Baron West of Cowie, meets strong head winds and opposition and is disinherited by his family and excommunicated from his church. The two lovers feel they have been abandoned and become even closer, accepting that they have tied their fate to each other. They are aware that negotiating this new landscape will be difficult.

Sitting alone in his empty house, Isaiah is tormented by the absence of his daughter. His sons now in a neighboring country, the death of his first born, and the anguish of having lost Ledicia, have created many questions about his life. What rises up is a force he cannot control. The driving reality of his life for all these years, now feels hollow. He is facing an existential reckoning. He knows how hard it will be for Simca and Edward to support themselves. The notion that he has abandoned his daughter to such a fate sits heavily on his conscience. He knows Ledicia would never allow this. Finally in order to rid himself of the guilt and pain he feels, he writes a letter hoping it will reach his daughter. In it he says he will take the long journey to see them, hoping he will be welcome.

Catching a merchant ship in the harbor that is willing to accept him as a passenger, he heads for London, a journey that is long and tedious. Once in London, he finds a coach that will take him to the small hamlet in Cornwall where Simca and Edward are living. He endures another two weeks on the road, by which time he is exhausted, sometimes finding he cannot catch his breath. He assumes it is due to the long time at sea and the dusty roads and does not take this sign seriously.

The reunion is joyful. He tries to hide his concern when he sees the homely cottage where they live. But Simca seems happier than he has ever seen her. Edward has found work in the tin mines which is hard aching work and doesn't pay well. Simca has bought a spinning wheel and spins wool and takes in embroidery assignments when they come along.

Seeing how industrious they both are, Isaiah decides to give them what money he has been saving so they can buy a small farm. The farm they choose is nestled attractively by an expanse of fields and rolling hills overlooking the rocky bluffs that line the shore. It is situated five miles outside of town. Edward is enthusiastic about becoming a sheep farmer and enjoys the company of his father-in-law. Simca is preparing to spin the wool their sheep will supply. They will also sell the raw bundles of wool they shear from their flock.

Isaiah left Edirne, thinking he would stay for only a short while, but he wants to stay with the young couple till they are settled.

For months the three of them live together and fix the small cottage on the farm's beautiful acres. There are windows to replace. The fireplace needs to be repointed and they cover the dirt floor with brick from the local foundry. The roof is rethatched. They are able to buy a flock of sheep and have enough land for them to graze. The townspeople help them build a barn and shearing pen.

Letters from Turkey are beginning to sound urgent. Isaiah must return to his post. He reluctantly prepares to leave. The morning of his departure, Simca brings him a cup of coffee and gives him the happy news that she is pregnant. Overjoyed by the prospect of another grandchild, he steps outside the cottage door surveying the beautiful landscape and the barnyard now filled with sheep and a few chickens and a horse. On his way to bring the horse a pail of water, he drops to his knees clutching at the pain around his heart.

He never regains consciousness, but while in a coma, there is a peaceful look on his face, as if he is a satisfied man. He has the look of a man who has done his job and is ready to join his little daughter and his beloved wife.

Ariel's favorite possession, his toy wooden horse.

23

ARIEL'S HORSE

RETURNING FROM RUSE, excited by what she is learning, Beka is about to visit the only cousin on her mother's side who still lives in Bulgaria. She'd wanted to meet Vicki long before now, but she was in Germany with her husband working on a special project. So far, everything Beka is learning is rich in family lore, convincing her that she made the right decision to remain in the country for a while longer.

Arriving at the address Vicki gave her, she looks up at the cement façade of an older building. There are rounded corner balconies, big windows and visible cracks running along its outer walls. Like so many of the buildings she has seen in Sofia, it has the same look of discarded elegance, displaying the scars of the years of neglect under the Communist government.

Buzzed right in after ringing the bell, the first thing she notices is the fine grill work around the ceiling of the elevator and the inlaid wooden floor. As the elevator bangs up against the walls of the shaft, she holds her breath and holds on to the sides of the carriage as it ascends to the sixth floor. Relieved to reach her destination, she's pretty sure she'll take the stairs when she leaves. An apartment door at the end of the hall bursts open, and a pretty woman rushes forward, throwing her arms around Beka, hugging her without restraint. Vicki ushers her into a pleasant but small apartment.

Invited to make herself comfortable, Beka enters the large living room. Looking around, she is not surprised at how familiar the room feels. There are oriental rugs on the floor, and oil paintings depicting small Bulgarian villages and large fishing vessels that hang on the wall. This room looks like it could belong to her aunts, uncles or even her parents. Choosing an armchair in the far corner of the room, she is confronted by a portrait of her mother! She is surrounded by potted plants and seems to be staring directly at her. She looks lovely but rather serious. Vicki has disappeared down a hallway and returns with a tray of tea and sandwiches.

"Vicki... this portrait...it's my mother. Do you know who painted it? From the look of it, she's already been in America for years."

"Oh yes, I believe it was painted by one of your mother's cousins, Rayko Levy, done in the sixties. I inherited it from my father. Rayko used a photograph to recreate her likeness because, of course, he couldn't paint her in person. You may have heard of him."

Beka shakes her head. "No, he's another member of this family I haven't heard of, but that's not surprising. I've always been out of the loop–till now."

"He was a relatively well-known painter. He gave this painting to my father as a gift –a way to remember his sister, because once your family left Bulgaria, my father never saw her again. He was very fond of his little sister."

Taking a seat closer to Vicki, Beka notes that she does not have any of the features of her mother's side of the family and wonders why, until she remembers that Vicki's mother was Bulgarian and a Christian.

"Vicki, my parents spoke of visiting Bulgaria all the time, but never could. The restrictions on Communist countries were formidable. By the time the iron curtain fell, my mother had already died. My father had a strong desire to visit before it was too late, realizing he didn't have many more years left. I wanted to take the trip with him, but without warning, he flew here on his own. I think he knew he was becoming frail and felt he couldn't wait for me to free up my schedule. I believe that was the first time you met him."

"It was. We were all so excited to meet him, though by then my father also was no longer alive. Your parents were always so kind about sending us money and clothing."

"The time after the war must have been difficult for your family."

"I suppose it was, but I was a child, so I didn't know life could be different. But after my children were grown, and we were free to travel I realized that we had been living in a country that was not free. I was astonished to see supermarkets. I couldn't believe it. There was shelf after shelf filled with such a wide selection of food – it took my breath away. You could buy anything you ever wanted. Here things were often not available, and if they were they were severely rationed. Even roses, which Bulgaria is famous for, were not always available to us."

Beka is listening attentively, but has a hard time avoiding her mother's eyes, but is soon brought back when Vicki offers her tea and begins talking about the apartment.

"We were very lucky to get this apartment when it became available. After the war we stayed in the apartment that belonged to our grandmother. The Communists had taken over the country and were assigning housing to displaced citizens. Because we had a family connection, they let us stay in the family apartment along with two other families. It was cramped and there wasn't much privacy. Looking back, it was not the best of times, but we got used to it. After my parents died, I stayed on in the apartment even after I got married and we raised our family there. It wasn't till years after the Berlin wall came down that we were able sell that apartment and buy this place."

After spending an hour getting to know one another, Beka wants to move the conversation towards her objective. She asks Vicki what she knows about the origins of the David family. Vicki excuses herself, leaves the room, coming back with a large zippered binder that holds old documents, photographs and letters.

"Our grandmother gave this to my father a month before she died. I think that's because my father, Theo, was the only one of the siblings that remained in Bulgaria. Both our grandparents died within six months of each other. There is an account that someone in the 1940s wrote, I don't know who, with the initials AD at the bottom. It is the account that is in this binder. He or she must have taken it upon themselves to write down what was only an oral history of our family." She hands Beka the binder. "So here, look it over. This is some of that history."

Beka is surprised that there were so many historians on both sides of her family that had the need or foresight to keep a record of their family. Perhaps it was because they were a race of people, disbursed, due to the world wars and the years before when no one was sure if they would ever find a home or a country. She looks through the photographs, examines the ribbons, medals and certificates that fill one side of the leather binder. The story of her ancestors dating as far back as the Inquisition is written down on sheets of faded blue paper and tucked away in a separate worn cloth folder. The story unfolds like a time capsule bursting open.

Amsterdam, The Netherlands
May, 1492 The year of the Spanish Inquisition

Ariel grabs his favorite possession, a small toy wooden horse. His mother grimaces, telling him it's too big, and he cannot take it with them. Ariel continues to hold it firmly. She is distracted, deciding what they should take with them and how many things they must leave behind before they depart. Focusing on her work, she ignores Ariel for the time being. They must leave tomorrow, having already hired a carriage to take them to Lisbon, hoping the driver will show up. They certainly paid him enough.

The next day, the David family, bitterly sad, but with a sense of urgency, leave Toledo and most everything behind. The carriage is cramped with very little room for the six of them to move or stretch out. The roads are uneven, narrow and dusty until on the third day there is a heavy downpour turning the dusty roads to mud, making the journey slower and even more treacherous. Each evening they stop at a roadside inn or hostel, unsure if they will be served dinner or given beds to sleep on. Relieved that they are not met with much resistance, they focus on their main objective which is to join the rest of their extended family in Lisbon. No one seems to notice the lump under Ariel's surcoat.

There is little question about what they have had to do. The demand to leave Spain or convert to Catholicism is firm. If they stay, they must convert. If they refuse to convert, they will be killed. Since they have no intention of converting to Catholicism, they're left with no choice but to get out of the country, even though it is the country of their birth, the country where all their ancestors were born, died, and were buried.

They had a reasonably good life in Toledo, becoming quite well off in their merchant trade. A trade which continued from one generation to the next so that this family had become masters in the art of buying, selling and sourcing out goods. Actually, it was one of the few ways Jews were allowed to make a living. Now evicted from their home by the Church and the government, they are uncertain about their future, feeling as though, they are once again forced to be nomadic, just as their ancestors had been.

After a hard year in Portugal living in crowded unpleasant quarters and not having enough work to keep them properly fed, they witness with alarm, that the religious climate in this country is no different than Spain's. Once again young Ariel hides his wooden horse and the family travels north to Amsterdam, where they hear they will be welcomed as long as they stay quartered with their own kind.

It is their reputation for being expert merchants that persuades the government of Amsterdam to invite the Spanish Jewry to their city, believing they will provide a very positive economic contribution. The government is unaware that their open disposition towards these immigrants might pose a problem. This is partly due to the fact that they had not experienced the negative attitudes of their citizens towards the Jewish immigrants and the religious conflicts that might arise.

The David family traded in coffee and spices while in Spain. In Amsterdam they are able to resume their work easily, in large part because of the Inquisition. When Sephardic Jews were forced to leave Spain, they settled far beyond western Europe and into The Levant, Morocco and the Ottoman Empire. This created an international network for products grown in *those countries. Ironically, at the same time, in competition with Portugal, Columbus is commissioned by Queen Isabella to find a better route to the East Indies. He leaves Spain in August of 1492, the same year as the Inquisition, and instead of finding India, China, Japan and the Spice Islands, Columbus finds himself in America!*

While life is better, there are inevitable conflicts in The Netherlands. Some of the feudal lords ruling smaller fiefdoms do not always welcome Jews and place many restrictions on them. In this way the David family still find themselves dealing with the arcane feelings of the populace who do not favor non-Christians. However, the general government policy of tolerance helps to assuage these problems when they surface and some local Burgomasters even support the Jews by enacting laws which suit their own interest and line their pockets, thus allowing the Jews to flourish. The Davids' are very sensitive to the atmosphere in the country, and remain on guard, while they quietly rebuild their lives and wealth without ostentation.

Though Jews are enjoying greater freedom than they had known in Spain, they are still denied certain rights. They cannot hold political office. Though they are allowed to attend the university, they are limited to the study of science and medicine. They cannot become lawyers or teach and are excluded from trade guilds so they cannot learn a skill or a trade to support their families. But even here there are exceptions. In order to earn a living, they are allowed a range of activities; They can become physicians, printers or merchants and vendors of books, meat, drugs, jewelry and tobacco.

When Ariel comes of age, he decides to study medicine and is the first member in his family to become a doctor, which makes his father very proud. He is the youngest and by far the favorite son. The other two sons are certainly loved, but do not have Ariel's charisma. They follow in their father's business and the youngest sibling, a daughter, is promised to a family friend, who has become a printer of religious manuscripts.

Ariel, an avid horseman, taller than his brothers by two inches, has dark piercing eyes which accentuate his imposing stature. He is a man, most mothers in the community fervently hope will become their son-in-law. He has been in practice for over a year and is still unmarried when a message arrives that his oldest brother has contracted typhoid fever while traveling in the Middle East. The long journey prevents Ariel from traveling there to *personally tend to his brother. The family can do nothing but anxiously await the news they fear will come. And it does. Their oldest son and brother died on his 40th birthday and was buried immediately. A pall of sadness has descended on the family. Ariel's mother now only wears black. Even though grief and death are no strangers, his death remains a permanent family sorrow.*

Ariel marries a few years after the death of his brother to an unusual woman who is independent and practices midwifery. She gives birth to ten children, but only five survive beyond the age of six. Ariel's father, growing older, gives over much of the responsibility of the business to his middle son, who now has his own family of six. In the decades that follow, the David family continues to grow and for more than a hundred years enjoys a certain amount of wealth and respect from their community.

The first break in their well-established lives comes in 1622 when one of the David men and his family accept King Christian IV's invitation to move to Denmark. The King, aspires to build his own maritime fleet and gain a foothold into this lucrative trade. Knowing that the Jews of The Netherlands have established strong commercial relationships with much of Europe and beyond, they are welcomed in Denmark.

Earlier, in 1621 the Dutch establish the Dutch West Indies Company, an event that changes the course of one of the David's lives. It is in June of 1623 that Hyram David, the great, great grandson of Ariel arrives home after receiving a medical degree from Leiden University. The house is quiet. Scanning the empty rooms to be sure no one is at home he sits down and writes a note to his family saying that he will be sailing to the Island of Curacao. He will write again when he arrives and finishes the note saying he loves them all. The youngest and most free-thinking of all his siblings, Hyram's physique and light complexion make it possible for him to pass as a Dutchman. He has grown tired of living in the busy hustle of cities, and feels none of the pull of either his religion or his father's business. As an atheist he knows what a blemish he has placed on his family, so a month before his graduation, he hatched a plan that he is now about to execute.

Wanting to find his way to the warm lush island, he dreams of half-clad women, exotic fruit falling from the trees and flowers blooming year-round. He is ready to move to what he is sure is paradise. He's done his duty, studied hard and is now about to do something that will forever change his life.

Placing his note where it will be easy to find, he leaves the house and walks towards the docks. Finding a vessel that is about to set sail for Curacao, he signs on as the ship's physician and leaves his comfortable home and all his possessions, which includes a curious old wooden horse, which belonged to his great, great, grandfather.

After weeks at sea, the ship reaches Curacao's port. He disembarks but does not show up when the ship is ready to return to Amsterdam. In fact, he never returns home nor is he ever heard from again. "The Hyram Disappearance" is a story that has sprouted a variety of legends in the family.

"He went native and married an islander. His throat was cut by a jealous ex-lover. He became a wealthy doctor, pandering to the white settlers. Conversely, he lived deep in the thickest part of the jungle, practically naked, practicing voodoo medicine. And the best of these rumors is that he counted as part of his family, a herd of deer and a lagoon full of lizards."

A few of the members of the David family join the Dutch West Indies Company years later curious to know what life is like in the tropics. They are seduced by the adventures of Hyram and the rumors of the glorious paradise that exists in this newly-found chain of Caribbean Islands the Dutch have acquired. Then too, they still hold onto the insult of being expelled from Spain, so there is some satisfaction in learning that the Dutch fleet captured these islands from the Spaniards

One of the effects of the French Revolution of 1795, is it changed certain laws in other European countries as well as in France. These countries began to reconsider their behavior with respect to its people. Netherland's government gives the Jewish community complete rights of citizenship. The effect of this friendlier climate has the result of growing the size and presence of the Sephardic community, and the David family with it. Most of Hyram's brothers and sisters and their progeny, lacking his wandering spirit, remain in The Netherlands well into the 19th century.

Beka looks for more pages but there are no more.

"So, this is where the story ends? In the 19th Century?"

Vicki takes the binder and rifles through it and finds one last page. This one is not written by the same person. The writing is different as is the paper it is written on.

"Look Beka, there is one more page."

Sofia, Bulgaria
1890-1939

Unlike his brothers, Samuel David, a direct descendant of the first Ariel known, is a curious man, unafraid of change, and ready to settle down. The 19th Century is almost over and the devastation of the First World War is still an unknown threat. Life feels full of promise. When he receives a proposition to marry Zora, the daughter of one of his business associates, he decides to leave Amsterdam and move to Bulgaria to marry her. Along with his business associates, they expand their venture into a thriving real estate business from Vienna to Sofia. All goes very well until the Second World War rearranges their lives.

Just before the beginning of World War One, in the early years of the 20th century, Sultana is born. Sultana is the youngest child and the second daughter of Samuel and Zora, arriving 13 years after their marriage. Zora, feeling much too old, leaves the care of Sultana to her oldest daughter, Flor.

Even though Beka's mother, Sultana, is born with the proverbial silver spoon, she is not a happy child: overprotected and forced to spend too much time with the women of her mother's generation. She is rarely allowed to play with children her own age. Once she becomes a wife and mother and moves to America, she is not unhappy that her silver spoon has turned into a more egalitarian stainless steel.

Beka looks up from the page, rubbing her eyes. "Man, there is so much I didn't know. So much I still don't know."

Vicki has been patiently waiting for her to finish reading and chimes in.

"Don't ask me about our grandfather, Samuel. I never knew him. He died at the start of the war, years before I was born. He was, from all reports, a very big man. The photographs I have seen of him remind me of a Rembrandt painting. Something of the Dutch must have rubbed off on him. He even had blue eyes."

"My mother never spoke of him. It was as if he was missing or not a central force in her life. But it is Hyram's story that fascinates me the most. What could have happened to him? Do you think he went native? Do you suppose we have island cousins? I am intrigued!" Beka looks through the binder hoping to find even the sketchiest depiction of him.

"I doubt we will ever know the real story, unless we go there and root out whatever records may have been kept. However, there are some rumors that may have some validity. The one I tend to believe is that he married a native woman and had a daughter who died at the age of eleven of a fever. But who knows? His story seems to be buried in the fertile earth of Curacao. There is no trace of him in Europe. Apparently, the efforts made to find him came up with one possible item: the death of a young girl who may have been his daughter. But I do not know what he looked like except for that short description."

Beka pauses. "You know what? I think I will just make up the rest of Hyram's story. I'm going to assume he led an amazing life. That he found exotic herbs that cured the natives. That he became an honored medicine man. I want to believe I had a great uncle who long ago was a headstrong adventurer and lived, unlike any of the rest of us, a mysterious life, right out of the pages of Joseph Conrad's novels. I want to believe that I once had a little cousin who was not white."

"Why not!" laughs Vicki.

As they continue their conversation, Beka notices something on the credenza behind Vicki that she had not noticed before. There is something contained in a glass box.

"Vicki, what is that, behind you? In the box?"

"Oh that. It's the only heirloom that remains from the David family. It's Ariel's horse."

24

THE OTHER DAVIDS

*S*QUINTING, LINDA DAVID *holds the newspaper towards the light coming through the window of their well-appointed breakfast room. She refuses to wear her glasses. She is a fine-looking woman, vain, shallow and self-centered, who refuses to wear her glasses. The article holds her near-sighted attention. Reuben walks in and pours himself a cup of coffee, surprised to see that Linda is reading the morning paper instead of Elle or Vogue.*

"Look at this Reuben. The Mossad have captured Adolf Eichmann, right here in Buenos Aires. He's been living here for years! The bastard is being brought back to Germany and will be tried for war crimes."

Reuben snatches the paper from Linda's hand.

"At last," he says under his breathe, giving her back the paper. "That monster deserves everything he is about to get."

—

Though Beka never really knew him, she remembers that her mother worshiped Reuben and waited for the letters he would occasionally write. Ten years older than Sultana, he hardly paid attention to his little sister. He was a man who in his early years often found himself in the middle of one nefarious scheme or another. Sometimes these schemes drew the suspicious attention of the authorities. Time and again it looked like he might get in trouble, but as luck will have it, he always managed to extract himself from the venture just in the nick of time and averted serious consequences. However, the last of these business deals drew him much too close to the fire. His partners were arrested for falsely claiming their assets to defraud clients. Reuben's name was not listed as a partner, so he escaped the law. While he saw himself as blameless, he decided it was a good time to leave Bulgaria, particularly as there were murmurs of war. With his wife Linda, and his young daughter Serina, they boarded a ship for Argentina where he had friends who were willing to sponsor him. Eventually he established himself as a businessman and before long he became the part-owner of a textile factory and not unlike many people who arrived in this country from Europe, became moderately wealthy. By understanding the ways of the country, he took advantage of the loose laws and the abundant resources that were cheap and easy to get.

Sultana was just a teenager when she became an aunt and doted on Serina as if she were her baby sister. Feeling as though Serina had been ripped from her arms, Sultana was heartbroken when Reuben and his family left Bulgaria for a country she hadn't even heard of. She would not see her brother or her beloved niece for another twenty-two years.

It is not until Beka becomes a teenager that she meets her mysterious Uncle Reuben. He and his family arrive in New York for a visit. She has vague memories of that visit. The first thing she recalls is walking down Central Park South with her mother, entering the lobby of a swank hotel, where he is waiting for them. He is a bear of a man and hugs Beka affectionately, nearly crushing her. When her mother sees her brother, she bursts in to tears. During this visit, Reuben is very generous. He takes them to see a performance of Carmen at the Metropolitan Opera. Her mother is touched by her brother's gesture and ecstatic to be sitting in this venerable opera house. Beka is annoyed that she must put on her best dress and shoes but admits she feels grand sitting in a first-tier box. That lasts for about a half hour before she becomes bored and falls asleep. No matter how hard she tries, these are the only memories she retains from his visit. She can only rely on the one discolored polaroid of her mother holding on to her brother's arm with real pride, taken at the end of that visit, to recall what he looked like.

She does, however, have a few memories of Reuben's wife, Linda who was always described as a beautiful woman. Beka often silently questions the family's idea of beauty, but accepts it as fact. Up till this visit, she knew Aunt Linda only by reputation as a volatile woman who often threatens suicide to dramatize her displeasure about anything that she couldn't control. Well-suited for the fine life style she has become accustomed to, she isn't disposed to display an ounce of humility or gratitude. Beka's mother tolerates her, but it is clear there is little affection for each other. Even today, Beka can picture this stylish, perfumed aunt who displayed absolutely no interest in her.

Beka is still curious about the David family. She would like to know what her grandparents were really like. She hasn't been told much about them. Consequently, she has drawn her own conclusions, but that certainly doesn't give her access to who they really were. She was much too young to have any memory of them. The few pictures of her grandmother and grandfather tell her very little, except, perhaps, that they must have had good appetites and probably weren't vegetarians. The photo of her grandfather shows a portly man with big round features, and her grandmother's portrait is of a woman who might have been pretty enough when young, with a softness around her eyes that can be described as kindly. But her pose is stiff and she is much too heavy for her own good. Even her mother's sister Flor, who stands beside them in one of the photos seems to have adopted a matronly style. She, too, has a nice face and kind eyes. Interesting, that her mother, Sultana, turned out to be the real beauty in the family and remained slim all her life.

She can't remember ever hearing her mother talk about her brother, Theo, Vicki's father, though I am sure he was in her thoughts too. He married a pretty Bulgarian woman, someone outside of their religion. She can't recall her mother talking about any of the family except for her sister Flor, who she loved with all her heart. Being so much younger than all her siblings must have left her with the feeling that her brothers were more like uncles than siblings, her sister more like a mother. What Beka does recall is the day in 1978 when a letter arrived informing her that Theo had succumbed to a heart attack and died at age 74. Her mother grieved the loss of the faraway brother she hardly got to know.

While sitting in Vicki's living room leafing through the archives, Beka thinks about how many years have passed since then. Life, Beka remarks, is unfair because it's not long enough to make all the corrections that should be made. Yet she is here now, sitting in Vicki's apartment. The three-year old cousin, sitting on the arm of sofa in the only photograph she has seen, is now a mature woman with grown children. Together they are collecting old stories and pushing them into the present.

"Why do you think your father chose not to leave Bulgaria during the war, Vicki?"

"I suppose the reason he didn't leave at the onset of the war was because he thought being married to a non-Jew would save him from any sort of persecution. He unfortunately miscalculated, because during that time, the German army still held sway over Bulgaria, and he was rounded up and sent to a German labor camp. Surviving the war and the labor camp, he rejoined my mother and resumed life as a bank officer. He was always elegant and fit, and must have felt hopeful enough, after the war, to soon become a father. She throws up her arms. "And here I am!"

Members of the Jewish Brigade

25

HUGO AND THE JEWISH BRIGADE

FEELING HER SEARCH is coming to an end, Beka wonders if it is time to go home. Should she call Michael? For some reason she hesitates. She hasn't heard from him in a week. Dismissing the thought, she picks up the phone to call him, and instead of dialing his number she calls Elise, letting her know she is thinking of leaving and gives her contact information. She doesn't want to lose touch. Elise, excited to hear from her, cries out,

"Oh, I was literally just about to call you. Don't go anywhere yet. Guess what? I spent yesterday afternoon with your cousin Hugo. He just arrived from France. He lives in Paris now. He had no idea you were in the country and wants to meet you."

"My cousin, Hugo?" Beka says with surprise. Then laughs. "Oh yes of course. That's really good news."

Preparing to meet Hugo today, her excitement is building, as up till now she has only heard his name mentioned. She has no idea what to expect. The one image she has of him comes from an old photograph taken sometime in 1946 along with some of her cousins, aunts and uncles, all of whom were in Israel at the same time. He is the only one in uniform. Beka always regarded him as the most handsome of all the relatives she knew or had seen in photographs. There was some pride in knowing that she had such a bold and adventurous cousin who was also a soldier. In fact, he was the only one she'd heard of in her generation, or the generation before hers, that had gone to war. He had the face of a rebel.

It is this image she carries with her as she walks into the café where they plan to meet for the first time. Of course, that image is now over sixty years old, but she recognizes him immediately. He seems very serious and doesn't smile, though he gets up to help her into her chair and greets her affectionately. The first thing she notices are his hands. They are the same hands as her father's. How odd, it seems to her, that she always notices hands and finds real comfort in them. Hands seem to connect her directly to her family. The one most familiar thing. When she met Margot she saw her mother's hands, now Beka sees her father's hands in Hugo's, as she did when first meeting Petya. Her initial impression of Hugo is that he is serious and seems to be, well, hard-boiled. Small talk is likely not part of his repartee. He seems to be without nostalgia or sentimentality. Yet there is also a kindness in his manner that diminishes her initial impression that he is someone who has the capacity to be caustic. But at this moment Beka has the sense that he is pleased to finally meet her.

"I remember your father, Rebekah. He was the easiest of my uncles to get to know. He had a good sense of humor. And your mother! She was a knockout. You look a bit like her. Is this your first visit here?"

"Yes, it is. I came here to claim the family apartment. I thought it would be a good opportunity to learn more about the family. I must admit I was never seriously interested before now."

"Of course. You became an American! Why should we matter? The apartment…where is it? I vaguely remember it. We visited there a few times, but I was still quite young and to tell the truth, not very interested either."

There is a pause in their conversation, a silence that feels uncomfortable, neither knowing exactly what to say. Then they both speak at once. Hugo is asking a question about herself, while Beka jumps into the silence with a request.

"Would you mind telling me about your life? I know you were a soldier and that you were married and had children; beyond that you are a blank page that I would like to fill."

He lapses into silence that lasts for a while, as if he is only now remembering he had a life before this moment.

"My life! Unsatisfactory!" He clears his throat. "In some ways, disappointing, but at the same time, it's the life I know I designed myself."

Tel Aviv, Israel
1940-1950

Lize's husband has been dead for ten years. She spends the years after her husband's suicide trying to maintain a brave front because she is solely responsible for raising her three young children. Hugo the oldest, Gina her only daughter, and Benjamin, the one she pampers. Europe is in turmoil and any hope that she will ever find happiness again seems a distant, if not impossible dream. However, she is a woman who knows what her duties are and never fails to appear strong, good-tempered and determined. Her smile can still light up the room, but, for her, worrying is like breathing.

This morning she receives disturbing news that Hugo, her oldest son, left for Palestine illegally on the kind of boats referred to as coffins. At first, she lets the letter lie unopened in front of her, afraid to learn what it will say. Taking a breath, she gathers her courage and carries it to the chair by the window, feeling she needs to sit down. Bracing herself she learns that when the British stopped the ship from docking, Hugo and a few others jumped overboard in an attempt to avoid capture. Inevitably they were caught and arrested.

Both frightened, angry, and relieved by the news that Hugo reached Palestine alive, she is dismayed to learn that he has been sent to jail. "Well at least he isn't dead!" Her anxiety for him has always been uppermost in her mind, knowing how headstrong he is.

—

Hugo languishes in a clearance camp for a year. During that time, he becomes a Zionist, believing that he must fight for this country because Jews have a biblical right to return to their homeland.

Walking out of the compound, his confinement over, Hugo lights a cigarette and breathes in the hot sultry air. A year of his life behind barbed wire has taught him at least one thing. He wants to join an army and fight for the right to be a free man in this country. He is told he can join a regiment of the British Army and he goes to their headquarters to sign up.

Perhaps it is the way his father died when he was only thirteen, or just an accident of fate, but something has turned him into an idealistic, arrogant and clever young man, and the only member of the extended Avraham family that is willing to join a fighting army. He has the soul of a Sabra that makes him outspoken, brash, independent and looking for adventure. The Jewish Brigade, an arm of the British military, is just being formed and he is given the opportunity to join.

This newly formed group is drilled for hours on end, every day except Saturday in observance of the Sabbath.. At the end of each day, Hugo can be found smoking outside his tent, idly sitting alongside his brothers.

"We should be included in the their army, but the British are not having any of it." He says to anyone who will listen.

His companions are all young, strong and willing to sacrifice themselves for the cause. They want to have a country of their own and fly their own flag identifying themselves with the country they believe belongs to them.

It is 1939, and the British government is standing in the way of assisting them because they feel they must appease the Arabs. They create a policy that denies Palestine the chance to become a state and they have gone one step further by severely limiting the immigration of Jews from Europe. This policy is poorly timed, as it comes just as Hitler is beginning to gain ground in Europe and is working on his diabolic plan to create a master race.

The Brigade spends each day rigorously testing themselves by developing their physical stamina. But each day they are frustrated that they are not recognized or included in the tactical exercises of the British army. They want to learn how to be soldiers. They want the British to recognize them as a legitimate fighting force and allow them to train alongside their Army, particularly now as they have been getting bad news about what is going on in Europe. They passionately want to defend the Allies. But British policies aren't letting this happen.

It takes a few years, but in 1944 Hugo and members of the Brigade get their chance. Kismet! The British 8ᵗʰ Army under the leadership of General Marshall Montgomery begins a drive to force Rommel's army out of el Alamein in Egypt. While they have successfully decimated the Germans' tank force, the minefields that the Germans planted are harder to clear. The British, desperate for reinforcements, decide to use the men of the Jewish Brigade to aid in the push against the Germans. Now the Brigade will finally be in the thick of it and show their mettle. When the Brigade first arrives in Egypt, they assemble in the desert to listen to a radio concert by the Palestine Symphony Orchestra, sending them off to fight. The music envelops them and injects in each one of the young men, pride and the determination to succeed.

It takes time, but the British are victorious. During the clearing of landmines, Hugo carefully crawls along the ground in search of mines. He sees his buddy who is near him step on a mine and get blown to bits. Hugo is wounded by that explosion. Incapacitated by his wounds, he lies in the mud screaming for help or his own death, but his time has not yet come. Rescued, he is sent to a hospital in Cairo where weeks go by before he is well enough to return to his regiment. (Fortunately, none of the wounds he endured are permanent.) They are sent to Alexandria where he takes part in the successful invasion of Malta. When the Brits join the American Fifth Army under General Mark Clark, they sweep through Salerno and Hugo witnesses the liberation of Rome. Proud to be a part of the liberation, he relishes every moment and stays on as part of the occupation force in Italy. In 1945, Hugo earns a certificate that allows him to legally immigrate to Palestine.

It is because of Hugo's connections in Palestine that his mother, Lize can leave Bulgaria a few years before the sanctioned and historic exodus of 1948. Her children, Gina and Benjamin arrive in Israel, determined to settle here.

Benjamin, forced to spend months in an Israeli work camp, decides to return to Russian-held Bulgaria.

Even with his success, Hugo still has bore the feeling that he is considered the black sheep of the family. He hopes that now, because he has been able to bring his family to Israel, he will be recognized for what he has achieved. Strangely, no one in the family understands why he feels this way. They consider him a hero.

The day Hugo returns to Palestine, he joins the Haganah whose activities during the war are fairly moderate. The Haganah was originally formed in 1920, during the early days of the resettlement of Jews in Palestine. Their mission then was to protect these settlements from Arab attacks. It had become the main Zionist para-military organization for the Jewish population. After the war it once again became active, filling its ranks with members of other smaller militia groups.

Once the United Nations adopt a partition plan for Palestine, Israel becomes a state which clearly defies British policy. This action allows for the exodus to Israel of almost all the Jews left in Europe. Meanwhile, the Haganah becomes the biggest fighting force on the ground. The massive influx of Jews will cause inevitable wars and conflicts between the Arabs and the Israelis. The first war begins and ends in 1948. The Haganah are able to defend their new country by successfully winning the battle, thereby becoming the official army of the state.

Hugo, now 32 years old has spent most of his young years on the battle-field and remains in uniform till 1950, at which point, weary, he leaves Israel for France and later Spain.

"You were a soldier for quite a long time. Why did you leave Israel? After all you fought to protect it?"

"I can't say for sure, Beka. I was tired and needed a change. Israel was still not at peace and hasn't been in all the years of its statehood. I thought I might find some peace in France, but after living there for four years I was not allowed to get a visa because I held a Spanish passport. I decided to go back to our roots in Spain. Why not? There didn't seem to be anything for me in Bulgaria. Most of my family had left, and I was ready to settle down."

"Is that when you got married?"

"Soon after that. But I never quite adjusted to being a civilian. Out of some sort of desperation I took a job in a watch company. That's where I met my wife, Rosanna. She was a secretary and a very sweet lady. I wasn't happy working for that company, so when I had an opportunity to become the hotel manager on the Costa Brava, I moved there and took Rosanna with me. We got married and eventually had two beautiful sons."

He pauses again. Beka can see that something in his reflections has become painful to talk about.

He looks straight into Beka's eyes, as if he is about to confess, and then says, "You know, I wasn't a very good husband. I didn't deserve her. She was such a gentle woman, and I wasn't able to be faithful. We divorced after a few turbulent years."

Beka doesn't know how to react, though she can't help thinking? *Are men ever faithful? For that matter, are women?*

"Then one day tragedy struck. It was the worst thing that can happen to a parent. I'm quite old now, and yet I have outlived my oldest son, Nicholas. I have never gotten over that. A father should not outlive his son."

"Oh, I'm so sorry."

"I have never been able to accept it. He was a fine man and killed for nothing! Nothing! It happened in LaReunion while he was working as a state administrator. Shot to death by a desperate man who couldn't find a job. He was simply in the wrong place at the wrong time. Just like that, he was gone." Hugo broods over his glass of wine.

"Enough! Now you know the whole story." With that he calls the waiter over and orders another bottle of wine.

Grandfather Joseph and Hugo

26

"A Man From a Time Gone By"

S TILL IN THE café, with two thirds of the bottle consumed, Beka feels
ready to continue the conversation.

"I believe you were still in Israel when our grandfather died. I know
that because your letter telling us of his death circulated around the
family. You wrote eloquently about his last days.

"Yes, I believe I wrote such a letter. Let's see what I can remember.
It was a long time ago."

Tel Aviv, Israel
1946 - December, 1949

*Joseph, the patriarch, living alone in Bulgaria is relieved that the war is
over. His wife has died, and most of his family scattered around the world, he
is suffering from loneliness. He was always a social man. His nature was always*

gentle and playful with his children and grandchildren, a sharp contrast from his late wife. She was a force to be reckoned with, but he misses her. Now there is hardly anyone who visits him.

It is Joseph's son-in-law, Gregor, Petya's father, who is able, with his connections, to get Joseph out of Bulgaria by way of Turkey and Cyprus. At the same time, his oldest son, Asher, has been trying to bring him to America. After much back and forth, Joseph decides his fate lies in Israel and sets out for the promised land. He talks about it as if it is his destiny. His final resting place.

In the summer heat of 1946, Joseph arrives in Palestine, kissing the ground when he steps onto the tarmac. He is met by Lize and her children. Hugging and kissing and crying, they welcome him to his new home. It has taken a lot of geographic maneuvering to get him out of Bulgaria now that the Russians are in charge, governing with such a heavy hand. It is difficult for people to leave the country, particularly difficult to travel to Israel. The British still have a firm hold on Palestine, and do not want to upset the Arabs with new Jewish settlements.

Joseph is growing older but looks older than his seventy-two years, yet he has rarely been ill. He has lived long enough to have seen many altercations and wars. As a boy he witnessed the Russian army enter Ruschuk in 1877 and now he will live just long enough to witness the founding of the State of Israel. There is no question but that he will live with the family.

Lize's brother, Charlo, Beka's other uncle and his family arrived in Palestine from Cyprus even before Lize and her family, so they have already set up a household. Charlo's daughter is only five when they leave Bulgaria and travel to Turkey. They stayed in Turkey for a short time before they leave again, only to find themselves in a refugee camp in Cyprus, where they linger for months until their name is called allowing them to enter Palestine.

Lize and her children move in with them when they arrive and with the addition of Joseph, the apartment is becoming crowded. This prompts Charlo to send his young daughter Hanna to Jerusalem to study with the French nuns at Our Lady of Zion. Hanna's mother was taught by this same order when she was a student. Having been tied to her parents for so long, little Hanna is lonely and rebellious. She does not like being separated from her parents. The nuns remind her of penguins and she doesn't speak the language.

It takes only two months before she is expelled for bad behavior and returned to her family in Tel Aviv.

When grandfather Joseph arrives, they welcome him even though they are forced to fit him into the family's very tight quarters. Joseph remains endearing, despite his difficult ways, often able to disrupt the entire household with his religious old-world habits and quaint attitudes.

As his memory begins to fade, he often stops people on the street to speak Ladino to them, assuming they will understand him. Always an avid reader of the daily newspaper, lately he is showing little interest in the current news. But what alarms Lize even more is that he has stopped reading his prayer book.

The morning he does not come when called for breakfast, no alarm bells go off immediately even though he is usually up before the others. Every morning he is found sitting in the kitchen waiting for his daughter to prepare his breakfast and the start of his morning routine. But this morning he is nowhere to be found. Lize becomes concerned and begins to look throughout the house before running into the street hoping to see him; but the street is empty. She calls Hugo in a frenzy. Hugo, still in the army, takes immediate action and asks his squadron to assist him in a search and they obligingly begin combing the city of Tel Aviv. There is no sign of him until three days later, when he is found seven miles away in the town of Holon. He is brought back home, still very much alive, but kicking and yelling at the two policemen who are trying to help him up the stairs.

He refuses to eat. Lize tries feeding him custards and porridges, but he won't touch any of it. Weeks go by before it is painfully clear that he will need skilled medical attention and after a lengthy search for a place that will take him, he is finally admitted to a hospital. The doctors provide little hope that he will get better.

"Our grandfather was a colorful man, Beka. A man that belonged to a time long gone. He was part of the world of the Ferdinands, Chamberlains and Morgans. I can still hear him break out in a song for no reason at all.

'Rebecca, Rebecca, di Haim di Mayo Io quando ti veyo, aye mi desmayo' - which roughly translated from Ladino goes something like:

'When I saw you, Rebecca, I felt dismayed.' Etc. Etc. His conversations were often hilarious."

Tel Aviv, Israel
The year 1946

After driving for miles on very poor dusty roads, Hugo returns to Tel Aviv and heads for his mother's house, sunburned and dirty. He is greeted by his grandfather.

"Good heavens, Hugo where are you coming from? You've made yourself old, black, and ugly."

He sees that Hugo is carrying a gun.

"What is this gun that you are walking through the streets with? It's a big mistake, querida. Listen to me, they are going to say that Jews are bad people. Hugo, against whom are you fighting?"

"The Arabs, grandfather."

He looks at Hugo as if he has just been told that Einstein is employed as a cashier at the neighborhood grocery.

"Against the Arabs? It is beneath our dignity to fight these ruffians."

Just then the air raid siren begins to wail. Lize closes all the windows and pulls down the shades hoping to keep any debris from flying into the house. This is not the first time there has been an alert. But as the Egyptian spits fly overhead and begin to bomb the city, all the windows in their house are completely shattered.

"What's all this?" cries Joseph indignantly. Is it war! War! Well war or no war they are going to wreck our house."

Settling into life in Israel has been anything but peaceful but Joseph seems to be unaware that he is often in danger. He continues to do what he is accustomed to, never veering from his daily rituals. He is annoyed if he has to rearrange his day, which includes a daily trip to the corner store to buy a newspaper. Tucking the paper under his arm he boards a bus that always stops in front of the store. One bus stop later, he gets off and walks to his favorite cafe and sits down over a Turkish coffee, opens his newspaper and smokes his first and only cigarette. Before long, he will strike up a heated conversations with the elderly gentlemen that sit around his table.

When the conflict with the Arabs becomes intense, it forces the govern-ment to call for a three-day search for hidden weapons during which time they issue a mandate that there will be no bus service. When Joseph hears this, he is furious.

"Does the King of England know about this?"

"We liked to use a name of endearment for Joseph Avraham, *Papucho*. Soon Papucho began to live in his own world. He'd been in Israel for only three years when he died at the age of seventy-six. His funeral was attended by a few people. The service was simple and the attendees offered their prayers and support to our family. They also talked kindly about him, recalling his amusing disposition. It was a very dignified and loving send-off."

With that Hugo empties his glass of wine.

"Beka, I need to take a walk. Would you like to come along? Are you hungry?"

They both get up at the same time. Beka walks in front of Hugo, then turns around and takes his arm. As they walk out into the fading light of early evening, Beka is sure that this day will linger in her memory. This man, almost ninety, still walks with a vigorous step. His back is straight, his shoulders square, and he does not have an ounce of extra fat on his body. His conversation tells her how sharp his memory is and how clear his mind, but now he is an old man. She cannot be sure she will ever have a chance to see him again so she wants this time to last.

27

REUNION

For six months Beka has been gorging on stories told to her by the current members of her family and unearthing information from various sources. She has begun to feel deeper connections to all the people she never got to know. What a wild ride it has been and now she realizes she is part of a world older than some trees. Her clan was made up of people with strange names that had their own special voices and feelings. Some were timid. sometimes scared, most had love affairs and many experienced the pain of childbirth. There is the General who had a distinguished career. A great grandfather that helped prevent a city from burning. An uncle summoned by the king who tried to achieve Bulgarian neutrality during the war, a cousin who went native, a small boy whose 15th century toy horse, lies preserved in a glass box in her cousin's 20th century home. Ancestors who fled Spain during the Inquisition. Other families that fled Austria during the war, as did her own parents who left Bulgaria. Aunts, uncles and cousins who were among the first to settle in the new state of Israel. Too many unknown relatives who died at the hands of the Nazis. She wishes she could time-travel and have conversations with them all. Share a meal. Commiserate and acknowledge the pain they endured. Save them? Be present at their weddings, their funerals, and their births. There is little doubt she would probably not like every one of them…maybe not even half of them. But more than some of them would hold her interest and her affection and they all have her gratitude for having been.

Spending so many months delving into the past, she almost forgot she has her own life and future to consider. She's been swimming in a river of memories that have flowed beyond the banks of what she imagined was possible, and now that river may be running dry.

These months have had another strange affect. She has become lonely for her life back in the States. It is time to leave. At least for now. There is a nagging feeling that something isn't quite right. Now scheduled to return home in a week, she wonders what awaits her. She feels wistful, wanting once again to be among familiar places, but what is also building up is an uncomfortable feeling of foreboding.

Ironically the day of her departure back to America is the same day, just a year ago, that she flew to Bulgaria with Michael to begin this improbable task. Being away from Michael for six months feels like forever. In the beginning of their separation, they called each other daily and talked for hours, sent emails and returned impromptu texts. Lately, communication has tapered off and when she hears from Michael, it's only by a text and spaced many days apart. These are not good signs, so she decides not to alert him that she is coming home.

She'd forgotten how long the journey is back to the States. But the distance provides her with the time to re-orient herself from the place she's been, to the place she is returning to. By the time she reaches her apartment, more than twenty hours later, she is almost too tired to do anything but fall into her familiar bed fully clothed.

In the morning she finds a huge pile of mail stuffed in her mailbox. Had she forgotten to alert the post office? She wanders around the house noticing the familiar things she surrounded herself with, and the way they no longer feel quite as familiar. She needs to open the windows to air out the place and finds the double hung windows annoying, because they always stick and are hard to open. Finding herself comparing things, she'd become particularly enamored by the smart way windows are designed to open in her Bulgarian apartment. The apartments here are functional but not as beautiful. The buildings there had an old-world magic, even though so many of them were in serious need of repair. On the other hand, there are no radiators here that create a heart-stopping sound when the heat comes up. And she can read all the road signs and everyone speaks English, though she rather liked hearing so many languages all around her in Europe. She felt cocooned in that foreign world. The odd feeling that while she still felt like a stranger, she was in a safe place, not needing to be visible. She knows that isn't exactly true, but nonetheless, it's how she felt.

Though she's been home for over a week, having pretty much taken care of everything that was neglected for a year, the one thing she hasn't done, the thing she has avoided doing is to call Michael. Her reason is partially that she is afraid of what he will say, but also, she has to regain her footing now that she is back home. What alarms Beka is that there has been no attempt on Michael's part to contact her! After she allows two weeks to go by, she finally picks up the phone, knowing she can't put it off much longer.

"Hello Michael, I'm back."

There is a pause on the other end of the phone.

"What? When? You didn't tell me…or…did you? Well," clearing his throat, "That's great. We have to get together soon."

His answer infuriates her. She returns his response with her own. "Yes, we should." and hangs up.

He calls her right back.

"Look I'm sorry, you caught me by surprise."

"Apparently! I'm surprised that you haven't tried to contact me for weeks Michael."

"True, but neither have you."

"Yes, but I was the last one to text you, and you never responded."

After more awkward small talk, they settle down and agree to meet at a local restaurant the following evening. When she walks in, Michael is already there and greets her affectionately, yet she can see that he is uneasy. Nevertheless, he takes charge, orders drinks for the two of them, views the menu and gives the server familiar instructions, then directs his attention to her.

"Well, Beka! When did you get back? Are you home for good? How does it feel?

"Yes, I am back, well, at least for now. The truth is I am not sure. I've only been back for two weeks. My intention is to try and pull everything together that we have gathered. I did learn a great deal more in the last few months. Are you still interested in this project?"

"Of course, I am! I definitely want to get involved, but right now I'm a bit tied up with a project at school. I should be much freer in a month."

"A month! Really! You must be very busy." It's clear to Beka that there has been a shift in the wind. His behavior makes her nervous and a bit angry.

"What is it, Michael? What's changed?"

Michael fiddles with his glass of wine, twisting it around. His behavior begins to annoy Beka who is already as nervous as a cat. He shrugs, his neck almost disappearing into his shoulders and takes another sip of his drink. Looking sheepishly at Beka, he admits he's been seeing someone in her absence. Beka is silent. The news does not surprise her, but the piercing pain she feels in the pit of her stomach does. She gets up from the table, "Excuse me, I have to go…thanks for the drink." Gathering up her coat she leaves the restaurant without looking at Michael.

Michael finds his wallet and hurriedly lays some money on the table and rushes after her.

"Stop Beka, please let me explain."

"Explain? What is there to explain?"

"It's complicated."

"Complicated? I don't think so, Michael."

"Look, I wasn't sure when or if you would come back…and…" He stops himself, realizing he has no honest way of explaining how and what has transpired.

"And–what?"

"And–damnit, I'm a man. Things happen."

"No doubt. So, that's it? That's your explanation?"

"Look Beka, please listen. We are not…Constance, her name is Constance, and I are not going to elope! She's a visiting professor and will be leaving at the end of the month once the project is done. It's just that she is a good person and we've been deeply involved in this project, and well…without wanting to, things happened."

"Things?"

"Look, I have feelings for you. Deep feelings, but I never quite knew what you wanted. You signaled that you were not ready to make a commitment."

"That's true, I was honest about that, and confused. You're right though. I never planned on becoming involved with you. But then I did. I began to care about you…and, anyway, we're getting older. I mean, we're no longer young." She realizes she is beginning to ramble and all her thoughts are coming out without the proper context. "Look. You better try and figure this out. So will I."

As she tries to get into her car, Michael stops her.

"Please promise me that you will be patient. Can you do that?" and as he pleads, he tries to grasp her hand.

She pulls away. "I can't promise anything. I was never sure our relationship was real. Then I thought it might be. Geez, Michael, it's only been six months? Couldn't you wait?"

Beka begins to cry, thinking, *"Damn, I didn't want to do this."* She tries to stifle her tears, not wanting to show her emotions. She is prideful, trying to convince herself and Michael that she does not need him or anybody. She'll be fine. Wasn't she fine before she met him? At the sign of her weakening, Michael folds her in his arms in an attempt to comfort her. Feeling his embrace, his body close, she goes limp for a few seconds before remembering what he just told her. Pushing him away, she manages to opens the car door. As she gets into her car, she looks at Michael for a moment, slams the car door and drives away.

The following week is rainy and dull. Beka can't find one reason to leave the house. Wandering through her apartment, she paces from the bedroom to the den and back into the living room. She goes to the kitchen, opens and closes the refrigerator door. Nothing interests her. She can barely keep food down. After her fourth cup of coffee, she begins to feel sick and falls back into her unmade bed. Waking up confused, she discovers it's already dark outside. Another day wasted. She knows she needs to put something nourishing into her body. Finding a wrinkled apple that is one day away from becoming a mushy brown mess, she throws it away.

Walking over to the table, she stares at the multiple piles of notes and photos she has gathered. She picks up a photograph, stares at it without really seeing it and puts it down. She can't concentrate. It's as if everything has become completely meaningless. There isn't anything she wants to deal with.

"So, I had a large interesting family. So, what! Well, dammit, I don't have one now and I'm not even sure I have a life!" Before she heads for bed again, she hears a loud voice shouting, startled when she realizes it's hers;

"Weren't you going to protect me...love me, help me find my story? Well, here it is Michael–spread out on this fucking table, gathering dust."

Taking off and tossing her lime green chenille bathrobe on the floor, she looks at it with disdain.

"Why am I wearing that thing? Who gave it to me? I would never have bought it. Whoever gave this to me must have known that it would be just the right thing for me to wear now. It looks like my life feels!"

She steps over it and climbs into bed wondering if she should change her pajamas, but abandons that idea and falls into her rumpled bed, pulling the cover up around her neck. Fatigue overwhelms her even though she's spent most of the last seven days sleeping. She closes her eyes, starts to cry and eventually falls back to sleep.

After two weeks of living like this, she wakes up this morning with a sudden burst of energy, like a withering flower that has finally been given water. This time she doesn't reach for her robe but instead runs into the shower and scrubs herself till she is almost bruised. She combs her hair and finds a pair of jeans and a clean shirt. She opens all the windows and with bare feet walks out onto her porch and breathes deeply. The cold infuses her skin with life. Her lungs are thankful to finally fill up with fresh air.

Walking into the den where all her ancestors are laid out on the table, she notices the painted rock that sits on her sideboard. It's not a rock at all, but a chunk of cement with iron rods sticking through it. It's a big piece of the Berlin wall. Touching the chunk of concrete, she is captivated, realizing that this is part of the infamous wall that separated a city for twenty-eight years and caused many deaths. Now a small part of it is here in her den. She stares at it, touches it, noticing the intense bold colors splashed over its surface. She begins to feel the lives that knew this wall and were captive to it. Here it sits, displayed on a wooden tripod, like a piece of art, comfortably situated by the window, spotlighted by the rays of the sun coming through the window. It takes her breath away because it represents a solid part of other people's lives. She must get on with hers.

Unhappy with how she's been behaving, she takes a second shower. When she puts on her clothes again, she is surprised at how loosely everything fits. She brushes her hair which has grown long and gray. She covers her sallow complexion with some foundation and colors her cheeks, so she doesn't look like the cadaver she has made of herself. She cleans the apartment which has gathered an alarming coat of dust. Vacuums all the rugs and mops the kitchen floor. She makes the bed with clean sheets, scrubs the bathroom till it shines and places clean towels on the rack and ceremoniously throws away the lime green robe. Though her appetite hasn't fully returned, she drives to the store to buy some fruit and a couple of cartons of yogurt, a loaf of bread, and as she is about to leave the store, throws in a bunch of carrots and a box of raspberries. Pouring herself a cup of tea, she dives into the carton of yogurt, adds some raspberries, picks up a page from the piles that have been lying on the table unattended.

For the next six hours, she reads every page carefully sorting and taking notes. She examines every photograph and places all of them into a chronology of years. When she is done, she sees before her, neatly organized on the table, the partial history of her family. A few members of the family had a real impact on history. Now she knows for sure that her family's journey began on the dusty streets of Spain. Two routes led one family to Amsterdam, the other to Edirne, Turkey. Some found themselves in the city of Ruse and Sofia, Bulgaria. Others settled in the former Yugoslavia, a few in the glittering world of Austria. Others found a home in the peaceful country of Switzerland, others in the dazzling world of Rome. They landed on the shores of Nice and settled in Paris and some traveled to Buenos Aires. But, sadly, the last home for some were the death camps of Hitler's War where they were worked to death or gassed, and for others, their last breath was taken against a wall, snuffed out by a Nazi firing squad. Her own family fled to America, while others lived and died in Israel. This families' reach spread out over various continents. Among this flock are rabbis, painters, healers, writers, scholars, merchants, military men, moneychangers, business people. Some were closed minded, bad-tempered, and weak. Other lives ended savagely. Some were noble and brave. Many were not. There were those who lived ordinary lives, doing what they could.

Her back aches from sitting so long and her eyes are tired from the strain of reading for such a long time. Surrounded by these stories and deeply affected by the vagaries of life, she puts on her overcoat, needing to breath the evening air–American air. It's winter and the light is fading. She never liked this time of day, the twilight hours. She likes it less now. It always feels like the saddest part of a day. The part of the day she calls the in-between time, no longer day, but not yet night, always the time when unpleasant thoughts bubble up and tend to find her the most vulnerable.

Walking down main street towards the coffee shop where she first met Michael, she smells the inviting aroma of roasting coffee beans drifting through the air, but she has no intention of stopping and picks up her pace. She thinks she hears her name being called but assumes it's her imagination and keeps on walking. Startled, she feels a hand on her shoulder. She turns around, ready to defend herself, surprised to see that it is Michael.

"I saw you from the window…I tapped on the glass. Didn't you hear me call you?"

"No. Well, I heard something, but didn't think…"

"I am so glad to see you." He wants to grab and hug her but thinks better of it. "I've wanted to call you so often but felt I should wait."

Beka stares blankly at Michael, not knowing what to say.

"Look, we have to talk. Please let me come by this evening. Are you free? Don't say no."

Beka, realizing how profoundly she let her life fall apart in the last few weeks and how much hurt she's been in, dismisses any pride she has been trying to hold onto. She looks at him and nods.

"No, Michael, I'm not busy. How about eight?

∼

OTHER BOOKS BY THE AUTHOR

A Reluctant Life

This is not a mawkish uplift. The insights are striking and the prose is accessible, luminous and stark. Though the book is dedicated to the husband she lost, the author might have written it for all loving wives who've had to travel the same path, through the mapless maze of grief and finally into recovery. Anyone who has gone or is going through a similar experience will not merely read, but recognize this book.

Clara at Sixty

Clara is the fictionalized sequel to A Reluctant Life, a coming of "aging" story. Clara has reached her sixth decade, feeling marginalized and invisible. After the death of her husband, her search for love assigns her to only further sadness.

Best Friends

It is a book of letters that tells the story of two aspiring young women, Beth and Yvette whose correspondence span a period of twenty-seven years--from San Francisco to a return to their roots in New York in the sixties, where they are involved in the Downtown art and political scene of the time, encountering and befriending people like; Bob Dylan, Dustin Hoffman, Shel Silverstein, Phil Ochs, Sam Shephard, Anna Halperin, Timothy Leary, Andre Gregory, Spaulding Gray, Eli Seigel, Andy Warhol, et al, and ends during the eighties when their lives spun off into widely divergent paths, one of them tragically.

ABOUT THE AUTHOR

Yvette Nachmias-Baeu

Writing is Yvette's final career. She has been a registered psychiatric nurse, an entrepreneur, a professional actress, film-maker, an advertising producer for a large New York Agency, and an administrator at Brown University. Her first book, award-winning, A Reluctant Life, is a memoir about the death of her husband and the process of grief. Clara at Sixty is the fictionalized sequel. Best Friends, her third non-fiction book is the chronicle of a twenty-seven-year friendship, played out in letters. She is the author of several published short stories and poems. While born in Bulgaria, she grew up in Manhattan and now lives in New England at the edge of a waterfall.

Made in the USA
Columbia, SC
22 June 2022

62085995R00115